The Art of Getting Your Own Sweet Way

Second Edition

Philip B. Crosby

McGraw-Hill Book Company

New York   St. Louis   San Francisco   Auckland
Bogotá   Hamburg   Johannesburg   London   Madrid
Mexico   Montreal   New Delhi   Panama   Paris
São Paulo   Singapore   Sydney   Tokyo   Toronto

First McGraw-Hill paperback edition, 1982

34567890 FGFG 89876

ISBN 0-07-014527-X

Library of Congress Cataloging in Publication Data
Crosby, Philip B
    The art of getting your own sweet way.

    Includes index.
    1. Management.   2. Success.   I. Title.
HD38.C68   1982   658.4   80-26011

ISBN 0-07-014515-6
       0-07-014527-X (pbk.)

Book designed by Mark E. Safran.

Contents

About the Author

Philip B. Crosby has been a quality management professional for twenty-eight years, spending fourteen of them as corporate vice president and director-quality for the ITT Corporation.

He is best known for developing the concepts of Zero Defects and Buck-A-Day.

Now a management consultant and lecturer, he presides over his Quality College in Winter Park, Florida.

Preface

When *The Art of Getting Your Own Sweet Way* was originally published in 1972, I was surprised to find that the publisher expected me to do interview programs on radio and television around the country. It had never occurred to me that the kind of business-oriented things I was talking about would be of interest to what I then regarded as the "general public." I had thought of situation management as something people did within organizations, even though I did use several non-business case histories in the book.

On these shows, I began to come into contact with family managers—the people who run homes, work, raise kids, handle the money, buy houses, run garage sales, paint the bedroom, select colleges, and in general do all of the things that life is about. Some of these family managers were women; some were men. The main thing was, they weren't interested in the problems of business managers per se; they were interested in solving their own problems.

As we talked and as I became further aware of the patterns that were occurring, I realized that there is a very strong parallel between the business executive and the family executive. The business executive has a more professional organization for assistance. But the family executive has advantages that are peculiar to that organization.

So I decided to go back and take a look at the book from the family executive's standpoint. I wanted to bring some business logic to that difficult management chore, and also see if I could make transfers in the other direction.

The laws of situation management, for instance, all have specific application in family life. Much more than in business relationships, as a matter of fact. One special thing encircles the family: the tie that binds is more enduring than that found in business. I know from personal experience that you can leave a company situation that was the absolute center of your life for many years and very soon find that you have a blank spot on your tape. Very little memory of anything except a few people.

The serial number, the form names, the branch office telephone number have all disappeared. The awareness of the current political situations disappears quickly and without comment. Nothing becomes dull more quickly than a conversation with old fellow employees who bring you up to date on the big problems at the company. Where once you would have hung on every word, now you find it difficult to retain interest.

It really doesn't matter to you anymore who becomes regional vice president. Unless you retained some stock in the company, you probably don't even care about the financial picture. The causes of caring are gone, forever.

But a family? Even when they aren't speaking, don't see each other, and have nothing in common anymore, they still care what happens. There is no way to stop it, even if you want to. All of that is not because of genetic distribution; it is because we have learned that family ties are enduring. We know it even if it doesn't seem true at that moment.

All of this means that family life and management may be more important than anything else. As I began to prepare the second edition of this book, I thought it might be fun to take some family situations that fit and describe them in the "situation analysis and prevention" manner. Once I got involved in the "fun" of putting family situations where business situations existed before, I found that the process took on different meaning. It became more serious.

Please don't tell anyone in the business community that I said this, but business management is not really that important. Every business I ever saw was managed below its potential. The wrong person gets promoted over the right person time and again, but it really doesn't seem to matter in the final analysis. Thousands of companies turn belly up every year, and life still goes on.

Government? Well, that is different, but only at the very top level. An erroneous assumption or decision by the top person can eliminate all of us. Most wars were the result of misjudgments or ego rather than the careful assessment of existing data. What the bureaucrats do or don't do every day makes little difference, but the person with the finger on the button is a horse of a different color.

Family matters are important because real things relating to real people are involved. The impressions laid on one individual can rattle along through a half dozen generations in one way or another.

So I hope you will take the concepts of *Sweet Way* seriously. You might be the person the world has been looking for to produce a little peace, quiet, and progress.

Philip Crosby
Winter Park, Florida

The Concept of Situation Management

People are raised to believe that things just happen to them and there isn't much they can do about it. They concentrate on a specific field in order to earn a living and provide a purpose for their existence. When situations arise outside of this specific field, they feel a lack of expertise and just handle things as best they can. Usually this results in losing a little ground each time. It is such results that develop cynicism.

However, it doesn't have to be like that. The management of situations can be handled quite easily by anyone who is willing to follow a logical thought pattern. This pattern is not difficult to learn and may be rehearsed to perfection by application within the person's acknowledged field of competence. The resulting successes supply a confidence factor, so the pattern can then be applied in situations where competence was not previously felt.

Situations only involve people, and people are not all that complicated concerning their wants and actions. They just want their own sweet way.

Situation Managers get their own way and have other people want that to happen by remaining calm and unemotional, while following their logical program. Getting your own sweet way is doing what you want to do and having everyone happy that things are turning out so well for you.

Introduction to Situation Management

You have probably noticed that the world was not designed specifically for you. Each day we must attend to the struggle of adjusting ourselves to the world or the world to ourselves. This is not necessarily an unenjoyable process. Life can be happy, purposeful, and pleasant. The only requirement is that we successfully resolve the situations continually presented to us by our social, business, political, familial, and physical environments.

The success average we maintain in this activity determines the amount of happiness, purposefulness, and pleasantness we will enjoy. Thus Situation Management is a vital tool.

We all manage for a living, whether it be getting a family out the door in the morning or manipulating an international financial deal. Because of this, the Situation Manager must develop a logical, repeatable method of resolving each difficulty, while at the same time turning it all to personal advantage. The best way, of course, is learning how to prevent a problem from happening in the first place.

Prevention is more difficult to learn. Extrication from situations by one means or another is somewhat instinctive. For better or worse, the whole thing will eventually end. That is because we are involved with the present, or the "now." But prevention is a future consideration, and if we are to prevent, we must recognize the potential for a difficult situation to occur. This requires a personal acceptance of vulnerability that is contrary to the inborn sense of immortality that each of us carries. Therefore, the approach must be systematic and disciplined, or we won't do it.

What are situations?

They are conditions that cause people to be faced with action decisions in order to return their life to its status prior to the condition. The action decisions people make and the actions they take determine whether the eventual result will increase or decrease their personal satisfaction with life.

Situations are opportunities for success; so are they opportunities for failure. While the overwhelming majority of situations can be understood and handled by people who are willing to give them proper thought, some situations cannot. Someone falling overboard in the middle of the night might be stumped for an effective action as the ship sails out of sight and the sharks move closer.

However, those faced with a misinformed boss, an irate spouse, an unlockable suitcase, or a broken promise know that it will be solved somehow. Their concern is to have it resolved in their favor, regularly.

To learn how to accomplish this, we must delve into the intricacies of Situation Management.

The problem we face in becoming effective Situation Managers is the same challenge presented in all aspects of our daily life: How do we learn quickly enough by experience and education to handle all possible situations?

The computer programmer, bus driver, machinist, secretary, executive, builder, banker, soldier, taxi driver, stockbroker, engineer, pilot, administrator, scientist, plumber, elder, minister, Democrat, Republican, golfer, wife, husband, father, mother, sister, brother, aunt, uncle, politician, etc., must learn to handle situations caused by other computer programmers, bus drivers, and on and on.

The difficulty of resolving situations comes from two basic causes:

1. None of us is only one thing. We are a combination of many occupations, responsibilities, and desires.

2. Most adverse situations are, at least in part, created by ourselves.

Because of these two characteristics, we tend to view each situation defensively and concentrate our first efforts on showing that we are indeed innocent victims of the inefficiencies or malevolences of others. Consider:

1. You double-park for 2 minutes in front of the cleaners and return in a rush only to find a $15 ticket on your car. You note that adequate parking has not been provided, that you had no other choice, and that obvious traffic violations are being committed all around you. You are upset that you have been thus picked on.

2. You go to your favorite restaurant with an important guest. The maitre d' greets you by name, but confesses that without a reservation you cannot be seated. Yet there are tables open, as you can plainly see. You are hurt at this ingratitude and embarrassed by the necessity to seek another place. It seems that this restaurant should take better care of its old customers.

3. The production department promised to deliver some equipment by the end of the month, and you have given the customer your word on it.

Then you find out that it wasn't shipped. You berate the production people, and they tell you that there was a good reason. You know that the reason can't be good enough. Why did they let you down?

4. You are driving along a deserted road late at night. Suddenly you have a blowout. The spare turns out to be flat also. As you stumble 3 miles through the dark, you rehearse a speech to your service-station manager. Why are they so irresponsible?

These are all situations that can happen or have happened to each of us. Our reaction is typical and predictable. The real question seems to be one concerning the "rights of man." Certainly a noble and profound subject. Extensive discussion of that particular point in any of these situations would produce a complete stand-off and quite possibly a revolution. Revolutions, or their encouragement, are avoided in management situations because they seem to reproduce the exact situation that existed prior to upheaval. They merely postpone resolution of the situation.

What we are concerned with here are two aspects: (1) how to extricate ourselves from the present condition we find ourselves facing, and (2) how to prevent such situations from engulfing us by never getting into them in the first place.

Let's apply those thoughts to the situations described:

Situation 1

Extrication. Pay the $15 and send the receipt to the cleaners with a suggestion that they provide adequate parking or provide free delivery service. They may repay you. But remember that you parked the car.

Prevention. Select cleaners that have adequate parking in the first place.

Situation 2

Extrication. Slip the maitre d' $10 while being gracious about it, and humbly state that you'll remember to make a reservation next time. Whether you go back there again is a different thing, but it is better not to expose your inadequacies to your guest.

Prevention. When you make a luncheon appointment, routinely make a reservation. You know that is the way to operate; otherwise, resign yourself to adding $10 to each lunch bill.

Situation 3

Extrication. Let the production people tell you the reason. It might be that the customer wanted a last-minute change, that the plant went on strike, or even that the product didn't work. If the reason is good enough to let them break their promise to you, it is probably good enough for you to use on the customer. If it isn't good enough, then take the production manager with you while you explain. He or she will learn a good lesson, and the customer will be flattered by the attention.

Prevention. People who make promises based on second-hand information deserve what happens to them. You gave your word quite casually. You should have looked at production's plans and schedules first in order to assure yourself that they had adequate time to handle any disasters that might occur.

Situation 4

Extrication. You can drive with a flat tire as quickly as you can walk. If you go slowly enough, the tire will last for 10 or 15 miles and you'll at least have light and shelter. If nothing else, stay in the car. If nobody comes along during the night, you'll at least have a fighting chance when the sun comes up. Don't make the situation worse by leaving the car.

Prevention. How did that flat tire get in the trunk? Make sure you weren't the "bad guy." How did the tires get worn enough to blow out? A flat can happen to anyone, but blowouts usually come from old or worn tires. No one interested in preventing dangerous situations can afford worn-out equipment.

If these discussions do not seem particularly earthshaking to you, you might try other everyday examples like "How can I double my money in the stock market?" or "How do I keep from getting soap in my eyes?"

We exist in situations. We manage situations. We are managed by situations. All we need to do in order to control our lives is to detect, understand, and resolve situations. Managers spend all day and most of the night working on their problems. Problems are their life's blood. However, very few take the time to understand the core of their problem. That is the difference between the managers who work their little hearts out and accomplish nothing and those who are truly effective, yet appear unconcerned. The logic of Situation Management can let you join the corps of the latter.

Consider what overworked business managers do. They read reports. They write reports. Reading has its own speed, and there are methods for increasing it that every manager knows. Those who spend their time going to speed-reading school receive their own rewards. But how about the matter of writing reports? Did you ever see someone burn the midnight oil to write a report? Certainly you did. Maybe you have done it yourself. Why does it require so much shuffling of paper, scratching of head, and correction of drafts? Perhaps because the writer doesn't understand the situation. How can you write about something that is not clear to you? Why spend so much time on execution and so little on comprehension?

If you truly understand the concept of Situation Management, you will be able to reduce your personal effort to a minimum. You will then have time to arrange your own situations and sit happily while others struggle to read and report. You can even be your own person.

The only managers this method will help are the ones who conscientiously apply Situation Management to the skills they already have. Obvious? Not necessarily. There are those who search for the easy solution, but as you know, there are no easy solutions—there are only consistent philosophies. Consistency wins, whether it wants to or not.

Situation Management won't make you a super manager unless you know your business. But you can know your business and still be a minor manager unless you consider controlling instead of just being.

There are only two kinds of managers: the growing and the obsolete. Unfortunately, the obsolete managers never recognize that they have reached this stage, although it is obvious to everyone else. The obsolete manager has had all the experiences and has a drawer full of available solutions, or at least thinks so.

As you become more involved in the stories described in the following chapters, you should start consciously applying the practices to your own problems. Start with little ones first and work up.

Situation Management is not like a tug of war. It matters not how many people are on each side. Your team will always consist of one member. You have no organization to worry about, no problems of requiring consensus on strategy, and no reports to submit. It is you, determined, fit, and resolved, on one side—the world on the other. That way, you can want your thing to happen more than they don't want it to happen.

Let's review the Laws of Situation Management first, since they provide an understanding of what causes situations to occur and an insight into the way people are going to react.

Then we'll explore the process of situation analysis, of resolving real-life situations, explaining each phase as it occurs. After that, we can review situation prevention.

Set your mind on open, and let's begin.

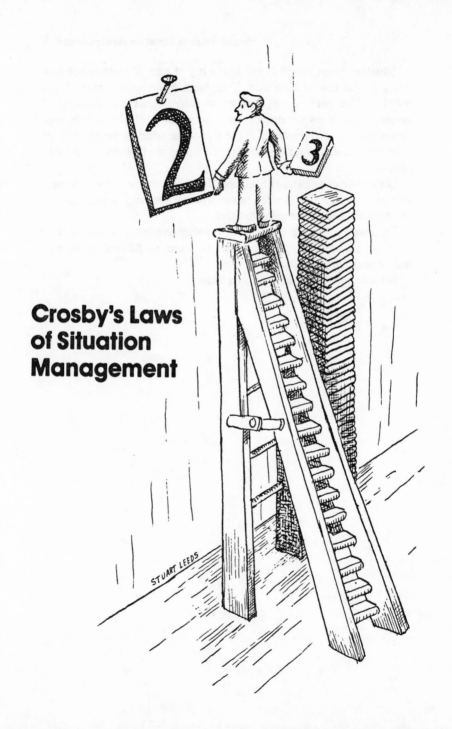

Crosby's Laws of Situation Management

STUART LEEDS

Since the purpose of this book is to prepare us to face a world dedicated to advancing further and faster than we can automatically comprehend, it follows that we should prepare ourselves to handle it methodically. The material aspects of the world may and do change. But people are pretty much the same as far as their personal concerns and motivations. Their basic actions in situations relate to the Laws of Situation Management.

These laws are practical guidelines. They exist to help you categorize the reasons people do the things they do and to provide guidance on the aspects of social intercourse that are important to Situation Managers.

If you study the laws carefully and don't fall victim to Law 10, you will be in good shape to handle the situation analysis and prevention activities described in the following chapters.

People are not complex. They just want to achieve their personal definition of peace and quiet and to have their own sweet way. They don't really mean most of the things they say, but will die rather than admit it. Their behavior patterns are as repetitious as their conversations. But people are what make the world go 'round, and we must learn to deal with them.

Crosby's Laws of Situation Management

1. The primary concern of management is survival.

2. Loyalty is a function of feeling appreciated.

3. The accuracy and completeness of information received varies inversely with the organizational position of the receiver.

4. The effectiveness of any program depends on the amount of participation delegated.

5. The less systematic support supplied to the decision maker, the better the decisions made.

6. Pride goes before all.

7. A job can only be as successful as the means provided to measure it.

8. People are more important to situations than things.

9. Improvement is the only practical management goal.

10. Nobody really listens.

LAW 1: The Primary Concern of Management Is Survival

There may be those who think this to be a law developed through cynicism. Actually it comes about the other way. It is a message of hope. Managers can view their own Situation Management activities clearly when the test is, "Will I survive this action?" After all, if the management survives, the operation will survive. There is only management so long as there is something to manage. This thought applies to nations, companies, marriages, colleges, or other legally constructed enterprises. Walk up to any department head in your company and say: "I understand that the board is going to petition to put the company into receivership." He or she will reply: "How do you feel that will affect my department?"

Approach your young son and state: "We are moving to South America tomorrow." He will say: "Will I have my own room?"

All that really matters to managers is self and the survival of that self. I am sure that many of us would turn ourselves out into the jungle and submit to a life of meditation, herbs, and loneliness if it could be proved beyond a shadow of a doubt that this would benefit the world. Because it cannot be proved, we must fight on to preserve that which makes us secure, since that is what will improve the world as we see it.

Survival depends upon controlling your environment, providing the image of achievement, and at the same time avoiding nonproductive conflict. Those who would muddle your world must be identified, analyzed, and disposed of quickly and cleanly. Violence is neither permitted nor encouraged, not only because violence is nasty but because it is not nearly so much fun as Situation Management.

For instance, a management's proposals to its stockholders must be couched in such a way that denial or modification of a specific proposal would not destroy the management. You cannot put your plans into effect if you are not there. If your whole program rests on a single yes or no, then you have little better than a 50-50 survival opportunity. You must provide alternatives that are equally acceptable to you because they achieve the same end, or else you may find yourself defending unto death something that is really not important.

You don't say: "The most important thing to me is money and if I don't get more, I'm going to quit."

You say: "One of the ways our company is measured by stock analysts, customers, and the public is the amount of money we pay our key executives. They expect important people to make important money."

The case we are about to discuss weaves around the joining together of two establishments of the business world, but it is just as applicable to the family world. You will recognize some of the people involved.

It wasn't too long ago that marriages were arranged in all levels of society. Sometimes daughters were married off to enlarge or protect the kingdom, but more often than not, it was a matter of gaining a cow or some farming right.

Romantic love is a fairly recent invention in practical terms—only the last couple of centuries, Shakespeare notwithstanding. The practicalities of life, when life was confined to the distance you could walk and return in a day, were not as they are today.

There doesn't seem to be as much made of it now, but a generation ago, we were always reading about some "cinderella" who married into a rich family or a rich girl who stubbornly married out of her class and was threatened by her parents. Those could be classified (by the parents) as "takeovers," which are prevalent in business today.

Each day people are married who obviously are not suited to each other (at least in the eyes of their families and friends), but they proceed with the merger anyway. Different backgrounds, faiths, interests, loyalties, and such seem to be cast aside in the overriding desire to be with the person of one's choice.

When the realities of a relationship assert themselves, when it comes time to go to church or go to the baseball game or name the child or spend the money or take the vacation, the merger has to be reconstructed on more practical and communication-based terms. As the management of an acquired firm must establish a base of understanding from which to deal with the acquirers, so those who become a family must form a base of understanding. If none is created deliberately and purposefully, then one will be created emotionally. Emotional bases are made of sand. They don't last.

In approaching a situation that needs to be managed or prevented, you must remember it is the final score that counts, not just form. While achieving this score requires keeping up integrity and morals, it does not necessarily require accumulated scars and wounds. If something is inevitable, like a merger, it is better to recognize that inevitability and utilize it to your advantage. The history of mergers in a free-enterprise community is usually that the company absorbed fights the controls and suggestions of the new parent company. And thus, after a year or so, its original organization and management are impossible to find. Some have been removed, some have left in a fit of pique, and some have just disappeared into the barely visible mist of "lower-middle management." (Lower-middle management is two levels below wherever you happen to be at the moment.) These tragedies occur for the most part because the individuals involved assume an erroneous and false pride that requires them to reject every suggestion, technique, or approach offered by the absorbing operation. They forget that the representatives coming to visit them are just as nervous about the situation as they are.

To make sure that your management ideals are the eventual winners, you must accept the proffered controls, suggestions, and inspirations in a manner that creates confidence and trust. You must become part of the crusade—the good gray judge who always looks at both sides. One of these days, they will move you into their tent, and you will have your opportunity to turn things around to the way you prefer them. If you do not survive, the opportunity will not happen.

Instead of waiting for an evaluation, request one. Then you can schedule it and probably even run the meeting. Don't be defensive; be positive. Some of their recommendations are bound to be good. But as you cheer them on, don't forget to price each suggestion. When the proper time comes, you can present the bill for all the improvements. If you get the money, you're way ahead. If you don't get it, no one can fault you. Perhaps the items were not made clear enough. Ask for another audit. Your stature will rise, the audits will continue, and nothing will change unless you wish it.

Let us return to the matter of the merger.

Big Daddy, Inc., an acquiring-type company, has purchased Outgo from its owners, the Outgoing family. While the family is in the counting house leafing through its new shares of Big Daddy certificates, the professional management of Outgo is suffering some concern. The key managers have gathered in the office of Outgo president Harold Hardwood to question their future. After all, the pay is good, and the work is not too hard. Who knows what will happen when Big Daddy comes in?

"Ladies and gentlemen," soothed Mr. Hardwood, "please calm yourselves. We will resolve this situation to our advantage, but you are all going to have to follow four rules. First, in our dealings with our brothers and sisters from Big Daddy, you must be open in all relationships and answer truthfully every question they ask you. Second, it is not necessary to volunteer information, because if they had wanted to know that particular thing, they would have asked you.

"Third, always say 'we' when speaking of the merger. Don't say 'you' or 'us.' Fourth, if someone provides you with a truly useful bit of information or guidance, be grateful. If they are impractical, smile a lot. That is all you have to do. Leave the rest to me."

When A. C. Bustle, the Big Daddy group executive, and his staff of four arrived at Outgo, they were met at the airport by Mr. Hardwood himself. Hardwood insisted on carrying A. C.'s suitcase to the old company station wagon and, puffing only slightly, drove the executives toward the Outgo plant. As they exchanged casual conversation during the drive, Bustle noted that the wagon had obviously been used to carry machinery, and there was quite a bit of grease splattered about the back seat. Two of his men attempted to wipe grease spots off their suits. "Don't worry about the grease," smiled Hardwood. "We'll get that off quick as a jiffy when we get back to the plant. We have some fluid that cuts the stuff like nothing."

"This seems to be a multipurpose car you have here," said Bustle.

"Only one we have," replied Hardwood. "Have to keep expenses down. I'm sure you fellows at Big Daddy feel like that too. Don't you?"

"Certainly we do, Mr. Hardwood. May I call you Harold? Yes, we are very concerned about expenses, Harold, but we also like to preserve a little of our image. We probably ought to get a less messy form of transportation."

"I'm glad to hear you say that, A. C.," said Hardwood. "The Outgoing family was so tight that I thought we'd never be able to get a decent automobile. I'll take care of that right away." He drove off onto a dirt road muttering something about a "shortcut," and it became too noisy for conversation.

The atmostphere at Outgo was most friendly. The fluid really did clean the spots off the clothes, and they all sat down to a plain but well-prepared lunch in the small executive dining room of the plant. The Outgo key executives had joined the group, and the Big Daddy team soon found themselves explaining all about the parent company, its plans, and its people to an interested and attentive audience. Every now and then an Outgo executive would ask a question to clarify a point and then jot the answer down on a note pad.

After a tour of the plant, the staff specialists met with their counterparts, while Bustle and Hardwood went over the general status of the operation.

Bustle was genuinely pleased at the progress he and Hardwood were making, until they reached the area of purchasing. Bustle noted that it was Outgo's practice to pay expediting fees on practically every piece of material received. "We have done that for the purpose of keeping our inventory low. There really isn't much room here in this facility to store things, so we've always just done it this way."

"That is the problem with a lot of management today, Harold," philosophized Bustle. "We do many things because we've always done it that way. In this case, it would probably be less expensive in the long run to lease a warehouse and place large orders at discount prices."

"I'll look into that right away, A. C.," said Hardwood, making a note.

That evening, the Outgo staff hosted the Big Daddy visitors at the country club to introduce them to the rest of their team. Bustle pulled Hardwood aside after dinner and complimented him on the arrangements and the attitudes of his people.

"However, Harold, I should say that this party, though well intended, is probably too expensive for what it will accomplish. You must always look at the return you will get for what you invest."

Hardwood thought about this for a moment. "I see what you mean, A. C. You sure know how to put your finger on the meat of the problem. I imagine you feel we should do something about our executive dining room at the plant, too."

"Well," smiled A. C., "I hadn't planned to mention it this trip, but now that you brought it up, I do feel that it might be better to have the dining room catered rather than to have a permanent staff on hand to prepare the meals. The food would be just as good, and I'm sure it would be less expensive. If nothing else, we would save on the fringe benefits we are now paying those employees."

"Good point," nodded Hardwood. "I'll take care of it immediately."

The next morning, the Big Daddy team presented its full report concerning the evaluation they had made of Outgo. Hardwood had made careful note of each point and stated after the meeting that he really appreciated the concern and wisdom expressed by the visitors. He promised a full action report within 2 weeks. The team was driven back to the airport in the same station wagon, but this time the inside was covered with bed sheets in order to protect their clothes.

Three weeks later, A. C. Bustle was called to the office of the Big Daddy president. "A. C., I have just received the action report from Outgo. They moved on every item your team presented to them, and there is a note from Hardwood taking special pains to point out that he personally appreciated the help and guidance you gave him. A fine job. I'd like to drop down there and see the place. This fellow Hardwood sounds like a very cooperative person."

When the Big Daddy president arrived to visit Outgo, he was driven to the plant in a new Cadillac. The ride was very pleasant, including no shortcuts, and the president found himself concerned with only one minor item: The seats of the car were covered with bed sheets. "To keep you from getting oil on your clothes," explained the driver.

Harold Hardwood greeted the president at the front door and immediately conducted him, along with his group, on a brief but informative tour of the plant. As they went through each department, Hardwood pointed out improvements that had been suggested by the Big Daddy team on its previous visit. He invited the department supervisors to comment on these improvements, and the president was delighted to learn that most comments were complimentary.

After the tour, they all settled in the conference room to discuss the aims and objectives of the visitation. They had completed only half of the agenda when Hardwood's assistant came in to give him a note.

"Gentlemen, our lunch is being served," he stated. "I suggest we go eat it while it is hot."

"Harold, can't we postpone the lunch for a few moments? I feel we are beginning to get to the heart of things," said the president.

"We can do that, sir," said Harold, "but there is no way to keep the food warm, and the caterers will take it back in 15 minutes if we don't show up. They can sell it in the plant down the road."

Lunch consisted of thinly sliced, warm roast beef, potatoes, and beans, accompanied by tasteless coffee. All of it was served on paper plates with plastic eating utensils. The caterer had left earlier to make his appointment at Valiant Industries, two blocks away. There were no napkins.

A. C. Bustle ate with his customary cheerful banter, but the president said nothing.

When the meal was completed, the executives returned to the conference room and finished the meeting. As the president was stepping into the Cadillac to return to the plane, he turned to Hardwood and smiled. "As I said, Harold, I think your operation is running very smoothly here. I am very pleased and encouraged. I feel that you and your staff have been most cooperative. All of you are major assets to Big Daddy, Inc.

"However, there are a couple of things that I don't quite understand—that horrible lunch for one thing, and this fine automobile with bed sheets in it. Somehow they don't seem to go along with the impression of efficiency I received from the rest of your operation. Also, I would like to get more information about that new warehouse you rented on the other side of town."

A. C. Bustle cleared his throat. "Perhaps," he said, "Harold wouldn't mind if I explained those items on the way to the airport."

"Not at all, A. C.," smiled Harold, "be my guest. And we will look forward to seeing you again in the very near future."

And they lived happily ever after.

Comment. The Outgo management will continue to run their company with a minimum of interference. The ground rules have been set. A. C. Bustle and his staff know that they can be more effective in other areas. I doubt that they will want to tangle with Outgo again. Survival was threatened by the merger. Counterthreat was poised. And the two canceled each other.

A couple of corollaries are present:

1. The most consistent survivors always tell the truth and deal sincerely, as far as anyone can tell.

2. A man with only one cow will never let it go.

LAW 2: Loyalty Is a Function of Feeling Appreciated

It seems as if every time I pick up a business magazine, there is an article or comment about the problem of the "transient executive." Prominent managers are quoted as saying that the problem of keeping good people is the primary one facing business management today. Then a discussion of profit sharing, stock options, and other compensation plans follows.

The purpose of the article is to show that top management, and their human resources advisers, are really onto the situation. They have identified the root of the problem and are taking the steps necessary to correct it. The solution, it seems, is merely a matter of providing the right amount of financial remuneration to ensure executive loyalty and productivity.

Apparently these leaders have never had a really good talk with themselves. Or if they have, they feel that the rest of the world is different. People don't work for money. They work for appreciation. Now, obviously I don't mean that executives or other people are not interested in money. Certainly they are. But their interest in it has little to do with the amount of work they accomplish or the loyalty they feel. Once a person is making a living wage and has some practical vision of security (such as hospitalization and pension plans), financial things are cast aside except as a measurement of recognition.

People usually don't change jobs just for money. The real difference between the $20,000 being made and the $25,000 being offered by a competitor is almost invisible. By the time a move is accomplished, the increase is all gone. Even if more money is involved, some lifestyle change will occur that will vacuum it up immediately.

Stock plans are set up for retirement or death. No reasonable person believes that either will occur to them. We are concerned primarily with the present, and for the present we want to be appreciated. Strangely enough, one of the least effective methods of showing appreciation is money. Of all the things money is, the main thing it isn't is personal. The numbers on a check represent no personal commitment or interest from the senior executives of the organization. They are just numbers. Money isn't money until you spend it. Just like a bell is no bell until you ring it (with apologies to Oscar Hammerstein).

If an item of recognition is not something you can touch or something that your peers can notice, then it doesn't exist.

We have all heard of children given everything by their parents except personal attention and understanding. Contemporary fiction is filled with stories of neglected children, heartbroken parents, and lonely grandmothers. Love itself is recognition and appreciation. Lack of appreciation can destroy it. Executives can feel unappreciated too, and when they feel that way, they start thinking about themselves and how mistreated they are. That is when they start polishing up the old résumé to embark on an industry-wide search for appreciation.

Box 3477
The Wall Street Journal
New York, New York

Dear Sir or Madam:

I am responding to your advertisement in
yesterday's paper concerning your need for an
engineering program manager. My detailed resume
is attached. I have been with my present employer
for five years. As you know, they are in the same
type of business you are.

Naturally you will be interested in why I
plan to change jobs. I could provide you with
several traditional reasons, but in order to
ensure that we understand each other, I should
explain something to you.

In the five years I have been here, I have
had a raise every year and my bonus has risen
proportionately. Travel expenses are generous,
and my relationships with my boss are good,
although we don't see each other with much fre-
quency.

But it is very difficult here to communicate
upward. There is no way to find out how you are
doing except by asking, and there is no way to
offer a new idea without making an issue of it.

Last month my boss asked me to cancel a long-
planned audit trip to make a special visit to a
major supplier who was having a lot of trouble.
It was difficult on such short notice to cancel
out and required a major diplomatic effort on my
part. But it was done. I spent a week at the
supplier's plant, and we got most of the problems
ironed out. I went back with a feeling of accomplishment.

However, in trying to report on the emergency
trip, I had great difficulty getting to see my
boss. He was tied up. When I finally got into

his office the next day and started to show him
the results of the visit, he looked at me blankly.

"Oh yes," he said, "I forgot to tell you.
We decided last Thursday to just cancel those
people out. They've been too much trouble over
the years. I meant to tell you, but it slipped
my mind. However, the trip was good experience
for you."

Now it is obvious to me that this is a company that doesn't feel it needs me very badly.
If I hadn't gone to see him, I could have been
working on that problem forever without knowing
that it was all over.

So before we start discussing my coming to
work with your company, I would like to make sure
that you have better communication practices than
these I have just described.

Very truly yours,

So far we have listed some of the things that appreciation isn't. What
are some of the things that it is? The most important thing that appreciation is, is the opportunity for personal contribution and the recognition
that goes with the acceptance or rejection of this contribution. Some
might raise their eyebrows at the suggestion that appreciation could be
associated with rejection of a person's ideas or deeds. Yet we have all
seen people struggle harder (that might be a good advertising slogan) to
overcome rejection than they have struggled to achieve recognition in
the first place.

If all else fails, you can resort to the use of professionalism. But first
you must understand, "What is professionalism?"

Why do specialists go to such lengths to require certification, examination, and oath-taking from those who would enter their profession?
Why do engineers differentiate between "degree men" and "practice
men"? Why do universities establish so many levels of titles, and why
does the military hang insignia on their people? To inform or protect the
public? To improve communications? Not necessarily.

All these devices exist for the same and sole basic reason: instant respect. The only titles used regularly are those which convey the bearer's status and knowledge immediately. You run into many "doctors," "colonels," "professors," etc., in your daily life. How often do you meet people billing themselves as "private first class," "merchant," or "room clerk"?

Parents take pains to make certain that their children call them by acceptable titles. "Mom" or "mother" are desirable; given first names are not. Yet grandparents will put up with almost anything. "Nana," "Poppop," "Daddy Ed" and so forth are not unusual. It is interesting to see some dignified executive, whose closest professional comrade would not think of calling anything but "Mr. Timpkins," responding to a child-given name.

Outside of normal affection it is said that grandparents and grandchildren get along so well because they have common enemies.

The point is that families are as full of titles and job descriptions as business organizations. Cousins, however distant, receive more attention than nonrelated people. In-laws of every description are accepted until proved unworthy.

There are many parallels between family links and corporate links. An individual belonging to a massive Fortune 500 company will immediately recognize the signals from another member of that corporation when they meet socially or professionally. They may tend to be more at ease with each other and may offer or accept hospitality that would not be given to a stranger. They are like brothers or close cousins in that they have their own disagreements and differences, but they pull together—at least as far as the outside world is concerned.

But to get back to the world of titles, let's remember that their sole purpose is to provide the listener or reader with a perception that is attractive.

"Gloria, I would like to present Dr. S. Lyndon Walker." Ah, romance and interest are in the air before a word has been spoken. "Vice president" used to be a pretty good status title in most companies, but now we have senior vice presidents, executive vice presidents, and even senior executive vice presidents. When introduced to a mere vice president now, people usually ask, "Vice president of what?"

Therefore, if you are to show your appreciation to those executives you would like to keep, you must take this phenomenon into consideration. A title is worth several raises, provided you make sure that other people understand the dignity contained therein. The truly inventive boss can keep everyone happy and recognized without much trouble if he learns how to handle the title tree. I suggest omitting regent, *führer,* and similar designations. They sometimes get out of hand.

LAW 3: The Accuracy and Completeness of Information Received Varies Inversely with the Organizational Position of the Receiver

The bigger your job and the more influence you possess over the lives and future of your associates, the less unfiltered information you will receive. This applies to parents and spouses as well as to executives. This situation occurs because of two beliefs held by every subordinate.

1. "It is not to my advantage to voluntarily tell my superiors things that place my judgment, competence, or actions in an unfavorable light." (This also applies to the parent-child relationship.)

2. "The superior has more information than I do, knows more about what is happening, and can do something about it. If the superior doesn't care, why should I worry?"

The love of accurate data has produced a whole new industry: management systems. The glamour companies of today are those that support and create management information. Computers, copiers, word processors, and software all exist because managers feel that they must have instant information. Companies spend millions of dollars establishing systems to automatically introduce all cost and service items into a central computer system. The information is programmed, analyzed, and transmitted to all interested managers.

Until recently, the only operations covered by data management were business and government organizations. Now, however, the home is being invaded. Each home has most of the necessary ingredients to be involved in_ electronic information. The telephone wire provides an entrance to every data bank, the television set provides the means to display the visual results of inquiries or commands, and a small electric typewriter or printer can complete the package. Naturally you will need a control package, but these will soon be available for the cost of a television set.

All of this will mean a dramatic change of pattern for the family. If information on all subjects, from the price of new shoes to local social activities, are available right at home in a satisfactory manner, the need for a great deal of travel is eliminated. Add to that the convenience of first-run movies and selected entertainment, and all of a sudden you are faced with everyone being home most of the time. (That will require real situation management.)

Data acquisition and analysis is something that family executives do continually anyhow. Through this systematized approach, they will be able to store everything from Aunt Ellie's personal likes and dislikes to the registration of each piece of property owned by the family. Birthdays, future plans, recipes—everything that passes between individuals or systems can be contained in the little box. Letters will be transmitted directly from box to box.

All of this might seem as if it would add a lot to the ability of the family executive to make great decisions about where the family should go in the future. Having all this information should give the decision maker a much better guide for making decisions, right? Not necessarily. Volume and organization by themselves add little to the basic integrity of the data.

Although it is both fast and bountiful, it usually consists of the same old filtered stuff. Output data can be no more refreshingly accurate than the input data from which it is concocted. Input data is always filtered. (Law 1 explained that.) To help us understand why it is filtered, we should examine one portion of the completed data package lying before the business executive. Suppose we take a noncomplex item—one that couldn't involve any filtered information, something straightforward and measurable, like finished-goods inventory. All you have to do to determine finished-goods inventory is count the finished items not yet sold or delivered. In fact, our mythical information system has set up a method whereby a card is filled out each time an item enters or leaves the finished-goods inventory. This information is put into the computer.

The arithmetic is completed, and we know precisely what this inventory is. Right? Not necessarily. Although the printout lying on the desk says that we have 34,182 items in finished-goods inventory, we really have 83,139. Seems some product-line managers have learned about "accruals." Accrual is taking credit for goods ordered by your customer but not yet delivered or paid for. It is a poor relation of the "float" system used by banks. The float system is something you may have been using without knowing it.

When you deposit an out-of-town check, your bank won't let you draw money on it for 3 to 4 days while they have it verified and do their book keeping. However, during these 3 or 4 days, they are busily lending out that very money, or money that it backs. They don't admit this. Individuals, when pressed for cash, will use this delay to let them pay money they don't have right at the moment but will receive in a few days. Checks that have no immediate substance but satisfy creditors are tempting.

A production manager faced with criticism for producing too much knows that the only way to reduce production is to eliminate people. Of course, once these workers are laid off, the overhead ratio (hourly rate paid versus salary paid) increases, which creates a new problem. On top of this, there is the sure knowledge that many of those experienced people will not be available when recall time arrives

This situation produces a cop-out. A portion of production is allocated to the turnover inherent in a large distribution system. It is there but you can't identify it. It is filling space that is thought to be used but never is.

Confusing? Certainly.

Think of it in terms of the gasoline tanks riding around in automobiles. If you took a measurement of the fuel in all those tanks at any specific moment, you would find the average content at half full or below. People see no reason for investing their money any sooner than needed. In addition, it is inconvenient to stop by the gasoline station more often than necessary. The fill-up signal is usually under one-quarter full.

However, if you start talking about a gas shortage, if you indicated that there will be long lines at the stations and that some of them might even close, then you have introduced a new system. Suddenly people don't like to have their tanks register below three-fourths full. This means they are stopping for gas three times as often.

More than that, it means that twice as much gasoline is now being stored in the tanks of the automobiles. If you figure an additional 8 gallons a car as a conservative estimate, then you are talking about a lot of gas—a potential in the United States of better than 800 million gallons of fuel absorbed and not used for fuel. That amount represents 25 percent of Florida's total annual usage.

Here is a case in which a prophecy is truly self-fulfilling. If nothing else will create a shortage, the announcement that there will be one will do it. The production manager keeps producing, but charges the units against the potential inventory flow. In real life, the boxes are sitting right there in the warehouse.

The top executives, poring over the numbers supplied by their system, are left with a feeling of contentment. The staff people, who know what is really going on, are unable to communicate this upward because they would have to explain why the system doesn't work. It is all very disconcerting.

There is a corollary to Law 3 that applies to a family as well as business executives: If you don't ask the right question, you don't get the right answer.

It is only fair to ask what the impact of filtered information might be. My gawd, what if the U.S. government, and particularly the Department of Defense, had to rely on such things? Can you imagine what would happen to us? (Ever hear of Bull Run? Pearl Harbor? the Bay of Pigs?)

No one is really bad. It is just that we all have different ideas concerning what "good" is. Each person feels that those receiving information require some assistance in interpreting it, so they place the interpretation in the report and allow it to appear as fact. Consider some examples:

"We are going to need twenty additional people to finish the work by Thursday." (Translation: I only need six, but you are going to cut me to that anyway.)

"Our customers are feeling the economic crunch and are planning on reducing their orders by 25 percent next month." (Translation: I had a lousy trip.)

"Engineering is working on a new design that will eliminate this problem." (Translation: We haven't been able to solve it here, so we are passing it along.)

"Tell it like it is" has become a slogan for the consumer of today. "Tell it like it ought to be" is the slogan of reporting managers. Let those who don't interpret cast the first termination slip.

LAW 4: The Effectiveness of Any Program Depends upon the Amount of Participation Delegated

No one can do the job as well as I.

Let us admire, applaud, and accept this statement. Now let us regretfully discard it. Anyone can do the job all alone but the ones who make the big money are those who can get others to do the job for them and enjoy every minute. (A la Tom Sawyer.)

We can all recognize from our personal experience that very few managers are able to accomplish this task. Things do get done, and done well, if enough attention and pressure are applied. But the only way they get done inexpensively, continuously, and effectively is if every person involved feels like a primary contributor, leading the way through example and accomplishment. In short, the successful manager knows how to create participation without making a big deal of it.

Let's consider two separate organizations. Each is interested in establishing a program to ensure that the purchases made in multiple locations are accomplished according to standard practices, maximum efficiency, and general all-around wonderfulness.

The first organization creates a new senior purchasing group. The group then writes a purchasing manual, conducts training courses among the purchasing people throughout the organization, and establishes auditors to continually survey the operations to be sure that the manual is being followed to the letter. The reports of the auditors are then circulated, and each responsible department is required to explain any lack of compliance to the manual. A training coordinator is hired. Courses are developed in those procedures noticed to be least utilized, and affected personnel are trained. The result is improved measurement of work activities and more unified purchasing operations, but lack of acceptance or participation by the personnel involved. They spend a great deal of time fighting the system. This means that there is much better record keeping but little actual improvement.

The second organization creates a senior purchasing executive who brings together those managers responsible for purchasing at the separate locations and presents them with the problem.

"Fellow managers, I have been asked to find a way to improve our effectiveness. Obviously I do not know how to do this. However, I think that together we can accomplish it. I would like your suggestions and guidance on how to proceed."

After a discussion, it becomes apparent that the steps necessary are to (1) identify the problems now faced, (2) determine their causes, and (3) conduct the proper system controls and training to eliminate the problems.

The operating managers distribute the assignments among themselves, and the investigation proceeds. A few months later, there is a large improvement at virtually no cost, and the improvement continues.

Why is the second method more effective than the first? Only one reason—it creates an environment of participation. This environment can only be developed through good intentions, patience, and delegation of responsibility. Strong guidance, little direction, and mutual respect are the techniques of participation. Specific direction, lecture discussions, and controlled training are the techniques of nonparticipation.

LAW 5: The Less Systematic Support Provided to the Decision Maker, the Better the Decisions Made

The industrial might of the world was built by individuals. They all possessed the virtues of strong will, absolute dedication, and determination to achieve some goal. They possessed some vices too, but that is not our problem.

These individuals personally controlled every part of their operation. If a decision had to be made on finance, marketing, quality, manufacturing, horticulture, or anything else—they made it. The measure of their success in making these decisions on a minute-by-minute basis was whether or not their company continued to be successful.

Today this system of management is unacceptable because stockholders own the companies and most managers are professionals instead of entrepreneurs. These professionals have developed management systems that provide volumes of data in order to help them make decisions (note Law 3). As a result, so much data is available that the decision is virtually made before the executive ever has the opportunity to go through the requisite pondering act.

The net result is: All decisions are made based on what occurred in the past.

Now, I yield to no one in my respect for the knowledge and experience gained in the past. In fact, one of my hobbies is trying to place stories from the front page of the Sunday *New York Times* at another point in history. Very little new happens in our political history. Only the names change.

But business events are not political events. Forms of government may develop, disappear, and redevelop, but forms of transportation are not likely to do so, nor is electronic technology. Henry Ford, Thomas Edison, Alexander Bell, and their like would not have passed a modern management system analysis. No precedents.

"But," you say, "I am not trying to create a new industry. I just want to determine the best place to move my family or open a new plant. Surely the information accumulated by the local utilities and other agencies will help me make this decision." Help? Yes. But the picture you get is based upon the skill of their technical writers and their public relations firm. After all, how many places are bad? There are successful operations everywhere, and right next door to them are unsuccessful activities.

What really matters is where you want to be. If you are there, then it will work.

Imagine the captain of a ship taking this step. Action is the captain's responsibility alone. Therefore, he makes command decisions automatically. Any normal individual placed in this position would be doing the same thing 10 minutes after coming aboard.

People rise to the challenge if it is given. Their nature, however, is to drop to the standards of the group because it is safer there. The more information available and the broader the chain of command, the larger the opportunity to pass the responsibility along. I have no facts on it, but I would bet that you can assess the achievements of any general or admiral by finding out which ones had sent the fewest number of messages requesting instructions from headquarters. Those who asked for the least help achieved the most.

It should be pointed out that the game is only successful when the consequences are serious. Those who make wrong decisions should be permitted to lose for real. Nothing sharpens the mind better than that.

LAW 6: Pride Goes Before All

Why will a soldier charge up a hill in the face of overwhelming enemy fire? Because he knows he'll get into trouble if he doesn't? For mom's apple pie? For the girl next door?

Hardly. He goes up that hill, hating every step of the way, so that he won't look bad in front of his comrades. That's pride.

What makes a production supervisor come to the plant in the middle of the night to make sure a behind-schedule job is getting done?

Why does a third grader sneak out of bed and work on her homework project by flashlight?

Why does a salesman bust his tail to go over his quota and win the contest? (It isn't the TV set he'll win.)

Why does a secretary make sure the boss's letters have no spelling or grammatical errors before they go out?

Why will 800 intelligent people, who obviously have better things to do, sit in an uncomfortable elementary school gym to watch 400 kids sing Christmas carols?

Why do people wear jewelry? Why do they discard their perfectly usable wardrobes to buy the latest fashion? Why are contact lenses popular?

Why do we want to fly first class, even though it is more expensive?

Orientals, practical souls that they are, have long acknowledged the importance of "face," which is pride. They speak of it frankly and put a lot of thought into not causing others to lose it. This prevents many embarrassing situations.

Westerners somehow feel that being concerned with self-pride is egotistical. They relate to "pride in work," "pride in country," and so forth, but "pride in self" is considered some sort of emotional sin. They have learned that personal concern is considered vanity.

By not recognizing it openly, they are therefore forced to many devious schemes to show that they are not motivated by pride in self. Boys aren't supposed to show their pride has been hurt. Girls must remain poised at all times. Fortunately this role concept is changing.

All of us are expected to endure stoically any of the personal put-downs that come our way. It is okay to react to physical insult, but not to soul insult. When personal pride is involved, people will walk firmly down a path that they know is wrong, and that they know other people know they know is wrong, before they will give in and let anyone know their feelings are hurt.

Since you cannot speak of your pride, or state frankly that your pride has been dented, there is very little chance that anyone will notice your problem. As such, the unsettlement sits there and boils, only to erupt when a totally unrelated situation arises to provide an opportunity for revenge.

This is, in my opinion, the prime reason for the high percentage of failures of marriages and other close relationships. It is often impossible to understand another's apparent overreaction to a minor but current incident because it is really a delayed reaction to something else.

To overcome the pride factor in Situation Management, you must force a communication with the other person—but on an indirect basis.

You don't hand people a bottle of mouthwash; you tell them about the wonderful one you discovered.

You don't tell people they are wrong. You give them a book on the particular subject, since they are well known as having an open mind.

Above all, you don't get involved with or disturb other people's prerogatives or mess around in their territory without a specific invitation.

Embarrassed kittens become tigers.

Fear of being left out, fear of rejection, fear that inadequacies will become known—these are the motivators of the pride that lead us astray. Because of these, the proud person may choose not to participate rather than face the consequences.

Before beginning to resolve a situation caused by another's pride, all good Situation Managers make sure that their own pride is not the one at fault.

LAW 7: A Job Can Only Be as Successful as the Means Supplied to Measure It

All bets are made on the first tee.

The successful Situation Manager is one who learns to establish the ground rules for success before launching into the job assigned. If nothing else, the Situation Manager must also decide what persons are involved in deciding when the job is finished and supply them with the means to measure progress.

Much of the tragedy of modern life is wrapped up in the failure to accomplish those two basic steps. Yet measurement is a normal pattern in our nonbusiness life. A golf course has 18 holes. A football field has goal lines. Parties have a time established for beginning and ending. Airplanes go from city to city. The list goes on.

Yet an amateur Situation Manager will accept an assignment to "go straighten out the problem in Cleveland" without establishing simple agreements, such as "What problem?" or "Which Cleveland?" Consequently, it is possible to work your little heart out and return to be considered inadequate.

You are going to be measured by some means, fair or foul. Usually the one doing the measuring has nothing specific in mind, so it is done by the seat of the pants. It is the situation equivalent to "Let's have lunch sometime." Careers are destroyed in this manner.

When there are no measurements called out at the start of the action, any of the players can keep score or call the game at will. Therefore, it is incumbent upon the junior person to establish the rules.

The situation in Cleveland will be fixed when what events occur? When what minds are changed? When what product or service is created that did not exist before?

If this rule could be established in world diplomacy, there would be far fewer conflicts. Consider the way it is handled now when the republic of AABAR gets upset with the republic of ZZAND. "You are not observing the treaty," says the minister of AABAR. "We are too," replies the minister of ZZAND. "You are not." Sabers are taken from the footlockers. Lights burn late at night, and the cabinets meet to contemplate the problem. AABAR notes that ZZAND has mobilized its guard regiments. Consequently, they put some gasoline in their airplane. This brings a further escalation by ZZAND in that they declare a state of emergency and lock up all who are opposed to the government. Each entreats the United States to help against the opposing forces of tyranny.

If some cool head in the UN asks what the problem is, that person is told the details of military preparation conducted by the other. The treaty, whatever it was, has been forgotten.

Any legitimate assignment must contain a definable purpose and a practical measurement of progress. To accept one otherwise is to do a disservice to yourself and to the person handing it out.

Of course, you want to be the one keeping track of the status.

ASSIGNMENT: Get a better turnout at the next PTA meeting.

The key item is knowing how many people were at the previous meetings. That way you know the number of members you need to attract in order to accomplish your mission. Make a simple flowchart showing what the attendance has been in the past, and mark your accomplishment on it. It will be obvious to the world that you have been successful.

ASSIGNMENT: Eliminate the problem of long lines at the cafeteria.

The key item, of course, is to obtain a documented count of how long the lines are now. An even more accurate measurement would be to determine the average waiting time. Then get agreement on a desirable waiting time. When you meet or beat that time, you are done.

ASSIGNMENT: Get a better grade in English.

ASSIGNMENT: Find out why Apex Machine Company doesn't buy from us any more.

ASSIGNMENT: A secret organization is trying to take over the government of Zambelia. Stop them. If any members of your team are killed or captured, the secretary will deny any knowledge of your activities.

LAW 8: People Are More Important to Situations than Things

In 1812, Napoleon marched his troops into Moscow. Except for minimum damage caused by fires set by the retreating Russians, the city was almost intact. There were, however, no people in the Russian capital except Napoleon and his group. Some days later he marched out again back across the frontier, hoping to beat the Russian winter and starvation. Napoleon had learned that a city is people, not things.

The same is true in the art of Situation Management. Things will rarely cause problems for you of their own volition. They do not have the ability to scheme, plot, or act. People, however, do. Things come and go (it has been stated that 90 percent of the things we use in our daily life did not exist in 1900), but people stay much the same.

Plutarch told about the conditions in Athens 500 years before Christ: "The disparity of fortune between rich and poor had reached its height, so that the city seemed to be in a truly dangerous condition, and no other means for freeing it from disturbances . . . seemed possible but despotic power. The poor, finding their situation worse with each year, the government and the army in the hands of their masters, and the corrupt courts deciding every issue against them, began to talk of violent revolt and a thoroughgoing redistribution of wealth. The rich, unable any longer to collect debts legally due them, and angry at the challenge to their savings and their property, invoked ancient laws, and prepared to defend themselves by force against a mob that seemed to threaten not only property but all established order, all religion, and all civilization."

That description could apply to conditions in almost every country at some time during its development. Portions of it apply to the thinking of some groups today. The solution was found by Solon, the man brought in to solve the problem of Athens. He canceled all debts, freed people sold into slavery for debt, and barred such arrangements in the future. Suddenly the Athenians found themselves with nothing to fight about. Solon had placed his finger squarely on the seat of emotion and with one masterful stroke wiped out the pet hate of everyone at the same time. The system was unfair. He removed it. Instead of material things, he gave them dignity and a new start.

Those who attempt to resolve similar situations by concentrating on material things alone would have set about redividing the land and redistributing the wealth until each person had approximately the same amount of things. Of course, within a few years, the distribution would become as before, since the smart or greedy always triumph in that aspect.

In our personal situations, we are always faced with the decision of concentrating our efforts on things (the computer is giving wrong answers) or people (the computer is being programmed incorrectly). Things are easier to manage than people, in the mind of the novice Situation Manager. Unfortunately, although things seem to cause problems, they do not express financial or personal gratitude once the situation is past. What is the use of solving a situation if nobody knows of your brilliance?

The mature Situation Manager goes where the action is. Action is something that pleases you, like money, appreciation, promotion, or recognition. There is nothing things can do for you that people can't improve upon.

LAW 9: Improvement Is the Only Practical
Management Goal

At annual report time around the management world, the call goes out for suggestions concerning goals to be accomplished by the organization during the forthcoming year. Said goals must be specific so that they can be measured.

I wonder what the stockholders would say if some of the following goals were submitted:

Reduce profit by 13.67 percent during the coming year

Increase salaries of all officers by 45 percent

Shorten work day but maintain current wages

Add 18 additional holidays

It is impossible that all these goals could be explained in a manner that would show them to be for the good of the company. If so, it would probably be accomplished by a new management team.

It is only practical to be concerned with improvement. To propose regression is fatal. All of this, of course, is a matter of our environment. We live in an age requiring bigger and better achievements.

We are tilted into the trap of needing to improve when potty training starts, and never cease improving until we are presented (not to our knowledge) with a bigger and better funeral than any other member of the family until then.

The incessant need for improvement is a disease, but it is vital for survival as a Situation Manager.

There is, however, one bright spot. Not all people are able to recognize improvement when they see it. It follows then that one may not necessarily recognize a backslide when it occurs. People who arrange improvement are called economists. Preferably they are employed by the party in power at the moment.

Losses were reduced by $645,729 during this reporting period

(Of course, we still dropped $7 million)

Therefore, if we are to achieve survival and triumph as Situation Managers, we must learn to look at everything in terms of improvement,

regardless of its total effect. Assuredly, the automobile was an improvement over the horse. Yet, if you are required to make a case for explaining why the company's vehicles were repossessed, you can come out for
smog abatement and declare that you are returning to the horse-drawn
van as one step in this direction.

Should the accountant abscond to Brazil with the funds and a secretary, you can point out that the overhead has been reduced by two
people.

But it is wise to recognize that no one wants to acknowledge the realities of lack of progress. There are times when such a lack may be the
best step, but it must be disguised.

Gaining weight adds dignity, like gray hair. Surely that is an
improvement.

LAW 10: Nobody Really Listens

"Stay out of that tree. You'll break an arm."

"Walk."

"Don't walk."

"If you carry your money in cash, you'll lose it."

"Put on a sweater, or you'll catch your death of cold."

"A penny saved is a penny earned."

"A fool and his money are soon parted."

"If you marry that girl, you'll regret it for the rest of your life."

"To get a good job, get a good education."

"Don't try to pet a strange dog. It will bite you."

"Do unto others as you would have others do unto you."

"Look before you leap."

"Neither a borrower nor a lender be."

"Marry in haste, repent at leisure."

"A torn jacket is soon mended, but hard words bruise the heart of a
child."

"An infallible way to make your child miserable is to satisfy all of his
demands."

"Never put off until tomorrow that which you can do today."

"None have more pride than those who dream that they have none."

"We flatter ourselves that we desert our vices when in reality they desert us."

"Few save the poor feel for the poor."

"What a man won't do for his girlfriend, he sure won't do for his wife."

"Never take yourself off the payroll."

And so on.

Santayana wrote, "Those who cannot remember the past are condemned to repeat it."

How strange it seems that with all the advice provided to succeeding generations throughout history, people keep making the same mistakes. The only difference is the broader opportunity for error offered by the advances of technology.

A young boy burns his fingers on the stove and looks tearfully up to his mother just as the cavewoman's son did after burning his fingers in the fire. After fixing the hurt, the mother is bound to remind him that she carefully explained how touching one's hand to the hot area would cause it to be burned. "You didn't listen."

How many people do you suppose have drowned every year because they swam energetically immediately after eating? Surely everyone knows that the food needs to be digested.

Speed is still a main cause of automobile accidents. Discarded refrigerators are still trapping little children. Bad accounting practices are still causing business failures.

There are volumes full of the wisdom of the past, and most of it is carefully read by each succeeding generation. Yet individuals still have to learn everything by themselves. Surely this is the cause of the perennial "generation gap."

There are two reasons why people don't listen: they don't think that the item under discussion affects them, or they think that their judgment is superior to that of the talker.

As a result, we career through life bouncing off that experience, hurdling this one, scratching our way over another, and continuing until we have gained enough wisdom to croak it into the ear of an unbeliever.

Situation Management is not about to change the nature of human beings. If people want to start over again with each birth, that is their business. Our business is to recognize that if we want them to understand something, we must work very hard to explain it, and we must be sure that we are reaching them.

You cannot take your message of wisdom and just hurl it out to the world knowing that it will be appreciated for itself and taken immediately to heart. You must make sure that your message has a personal impact on the life of the listener.

Obviously, it is impractical to withhold food or comfort until the words can be recited in perfect sequence. That not only doesn't ensure understanding, but may get you into trouble. You can withhold love or honor, but that technique is restricted by how many people care whether you love or honor them.

Recognize it. You must concentrate very hard to get a true listener. I hope that if you find one, you will be kind enough to share with me.

The Family
Executive

STUART LEEDS

One of the most persistent displays of prejudice within our civilization is against those who stay home and run families. Traditionally, this has been a job assigned solely to women, but now men are entering the field as young couples work out sharing situations. But even in these cases, an implication still persists that the job is somehow a little below the status of a "real" job.

Real management is only supposed to happen inside certified companies, corporations, or on the pages of *Fortune* magazine. The only management you can get paid for may come under that category, but the most difficult of management jobs occurs running a family. Business executives have it easy compared to family executives.

The family executive (FE) and the business executive (BE) have everything in common except public recognition and tools of assistance. Everyone knows how tough it is to manage a business or do any kind of supervisory function within that business. Colleges teach it, clinics treat it, magazines aggrandize it. Business schools have it arranged so you can spend your whole life learning how to manage. In fact, you can go right from final graduation to retirement without ever having actually done anything. If you manage your training right, you will never have to manage.

The family executive runs the real world, determining how a group of people will live, what basic attitudes they will have, how they will conduct their personal lives once they leave the organization, while at the same time managing financial, social, public relations, purchasing, production control, medical, accounting, and numerous other aspects of the family system. They learn truths like this one: Keeping neat records of overspending is not money management.

It may turn out to be true that we inherit our competence and behavior characteristics. Geniuses, soccer players, criminals may indeed be born, not made. However, a race car cannot win the race by itself. Someone must direct it, tune it, and place it in a position to exercise its inherited potential.

It is not my intention to get involved in arguing or defending the value of the family or in discussing the emotional aspects that go along with Mother's Day or Father's Day or, for that matter, even the new Grandparents' Day. (You might wonder why the grandparents, who are usually in a position to be more generous than parents, only rate one day between them.)

The family executive aspect of Situation Management is put forth only to reaffirm that management is where you find it. You do not have to dig out a separate set of rules in order to manage personal situations (as opposed to business situations). The only things that change are definitions and measurements. Consider how the laws of Situation Management apply to the family executive and to the business executive.

LAW 1: The Primary Concern of Management is Survival

Business Executive.   Survival is a matter of keeping control of the budget, not letting your authority be negated in any way, and continuing to have more information about your subject than anyone else. If you don't survive, you can never reach your management goals.

Family Executive.   Survival is a matter of keeping control of the person who generates the budget, setting up "gates" (through which family members must pass before they do something) in order to reaffirm your authority continually, and being the one who talks to all family members continually, thus being the authorized source of information.

Comment.   Businesses are packed with information. Staffs within the company as well as the business media compete to see who can provide the executive with information that will cause the executive to create decisions favorable to them. Budgets are set by committees, whether informally or formally. Companies can operate at a deficit if they wish, their accounting staff can keep track, and the treasurer can borrow more on the assets that the accountants define. If a budget is overrun, the executive involved is chastised, but life goes on.

Families, however, are not packed with information. Each member is a separate company and not likely to run up and down the living room volunteering detailed personal information once past the age of 12. Data must be dug out by the family executive. Budgets are not variable. They are based on the income of the family and allocated so that all the actions taking place fit into that scheme. Debt is a serious thing, since real people have to pay back real money. It isn't like companies, which can move numbers around for years until inflation relieves the debt. It has been said that if you borrow $2000 from a bank and can't pay it back, *you* have a problem, but if you borrow a million and can't repay, *they* have a problem.

Thus, the main survival difference between the BE and the FE is that the FE is always in charge of a conglomerate, and they are much more difficult to handle.

LAW 2: Loyalty Is a Function of Feeling Appreciated

Business Executive. Retaining the loyalty of the business staff is a matter of paying attention to them: Make sure that they are protected from the human resources department; obtain their raises on time; and always give them the opportunity to discuss things with you. Ensuring that you are appreciated by your bosses is a matter of establishing a positive, open relationship based on measurable objectives.

Family Executive. Retaining the loyalty of the family members past the normal emotional attachment stage requires dealing with them openly, with as little vacillation on standards as possible; protecting them from the world when they are outclassed in a confrontation; and supplying communications at all times. To ensure that you are appreciated requires that the things you do for each other come from the genuine desire to help, rather than the more common human condition of self-sacrifice.

Comment. The big difference between the BE and FE on this law is that the BE can go off and get a better job with more money and guaranteed loyalty. As soon as the body is transferred behind the new desk, all things are instantly in existence: staff, budget, lunch with the Board, the whole schmear.

The FE who wishes to change jobs is required to grow a new family all over again. The alternative is to marry an already existing family and assume command, but some of the situations that occur there can be worse than the original operation (unless you can get your own TV show). It is obvious that the BE has a great advantage over the FE when it comes to options of employment.

LAW 3: The Accuracy and Completeness of Information Received Varies Inversely with the Organizational Position of the Receiver

Business Executive.   The struggle to sift clear facts and truth from the volumes of information received is cluttered by the natural tendency we all have to keep information that does not reflect well on us out of the hands of those with power over us. Thus, the BE must rely on hunches and earlier experience to determine where digging deeper will be fruitful. As time goes on, the BE becomes less and less aware of the real things that are happening. This is the prime reason BEs eventually fail.

Family Executive.   All family members have at least half of their world different from the other family members. That means that 50 percent of their information is specialized. And, of course, they all have a natural tendency not to volunteer information that will make them look bad. Thus the FE is required to constantly keep in touch with all areas of the community in order to pick up enough information to open a line of questioning. Certainly in most cases, the FE can be among the last to know.

Comment.   The BE deals with blocks on the organization chart containing fairly standard people. A junior accountant, for instance, will always look very much the same to someone who only wants information from that block. Group executives have their own management styles and vagaries, but they perform a recognizable function and can be depended on to do certain things regardless of who they are. In all these things the BE can have some confidence.

But the FE is faced with an entirely different problem. All the members of the organization are at an age and in a job they have never experienced before. The FE is required to know what people of all ages are exposed to and how they should react to that exposure. The FE is given as little information as possible because it is well known that any data passed through will be acted upon. The FE cannot rely on the activities of the past in the way that the BE can. There is no past. There never was that exact 14-year-old boy who loved hawks or 35-year-old woman who painted all night or 7-year-old who wouldn't go to school or were there the hundred brand new experiences that occur on a daily basis. And, of course, all information is terrifically biased. It takes a natural detective to be an FE.

LAW 4: The Effectiveness of Any Program Depends on the Amount of Participation Delegated

Business Executive. Delegating is what being an executive is all about. If you don't delegate, then you are really just a supervisor working directly with the people and guiding their every movement.

Delegating is giving individuals specific responsibilities, making certain they understand them, and then waiting impatiently while they muddle through doing what you could do better yourself if you only had time. There are many significant treatises written about delegation, but, at its most basic, it is necessary and extremely difficult. Necessary because Eisenhower couldn't have invaded France all by himself, and difficult because all the work of the executive is aimed at getting people to do what they are supposed to want to do in the first place.

Family Executive. No place in the world is the phrase "If I want something done right, I have to do it myself" heard more than within the family. But the successful FE knows that family members have to learn through doing and that doing must be delegated, even if it means that the peas won't be extracted from the shells until 20 minutes after the rest of the meal is eaten. But more than a business, a family has to be a group of people helping each other, caring for each other by participating. If nothing is delegated, if each significant task except for fetching and carrying is clutched to the breast of the FE, then the family members will not grow. They will never be ready for more responsibility because they haven't had past responsibility.

Comment. The BE has the advantage of organization charts and formalized lines of command. Utilizing these makes life easier; at least it becomes clear where the blame falls. The FE doesn't have this latitude. If the job doesn't get done, something important doesn't happen. Then the FE will be forced to rush in, improvise, and thereby reduce even more the self-confidence of the individual involved. It is a difficult thing to do for the experienced FE, but it is necessary that someone be permitted to fail in accomplishing their delegated task without being rescued by the older set of hands. Helped, but not salvaged, might be a good measurement base.

LAW 5: The Less Systematic Support Supplied to the Decision Maker, the Better the Decisions Made

Business Executive. As we have seen earlier, you can be overwhelmed with information and guidance in making decisions. This requires that the past be a large factor in determining the future. Certainly it should be, but there is a large need today for an innovative look at decision making. People have to go on what they know plus what they feel. The BE must go through the formalities of asking for committee or group reviews in order to provide a cushion for saving face if things don't work out all that well. But to retain one's integrity as an individual, you have to make your own decisions, taking steps to convince others that they shared in your creation.

Family Executive. Unfortunately, most of the information your parents gave you is out of date or erroneous by the time you have the opportunity to do something with it. But no one receives more free advice than the FE, who is bombarded with commercials, articles, and face-to-face discussion. There is no subject not buried in 3 feet of information. Most of it, however, is self-serving and inappropriate except for use as a base of broad knowledge. The FE must make decisions based on a personal evaluation of how a given situation relates to the goals of the family, and of course to the goals of the FE. Nowhere do the members of the family gain lessons in integrity more than when the FE has to make a tough decision.

Comment. The worst thing that can happen to the BE is financial loss or damaged reputation, which can be overcome and repaired. The FE can make decisions that scar the lives of family members forever. Therefore, every family decision has to be attuned to the goals of the family. Conservatism is the order of the day. Very few long-range goals are important to a family because a family is continually changing. By the time you attain a long-range goal, it is obsolete.

LAW 6: Pride Goes Before All

Business Executive. Most of the really important executives you meet are super-polite and considerate of other's feelings. They will leap from their chairs to open doors, they will insist on giving you the best seat, they will always ask after your family. All of this is a reminder that they have learned that it is to their advantage not to jar the pride of their visitor or subordinates. They have learned to submerge their own pride a little in order not to expose their wounds. But never make the mistake of thinking their pride does not exist. The more sensitive they are about you, the more sensitive they are about themselves. You have to give up something to get to the top of the ladder and in the public eye. The successful BE knows that this subject is something that requires constant work. You can get away with a lot of inadequacy as long as you don't scratch someone's pride.

Family Executive. When you have a situation in which one person gives a lot more to other persons than they receive in return, you have a culturing place for hurt pride. This is the Achilles' heel of the FE. Standing solidly in the control spot of the family, the FE is a participant in each and every action that takes place (or is supposed to take place). As a result there is unlimited opportunity for having one's pride hurt.

Comment. It is up to the FE to create an open communications system so that the one who is hurt can speak up and have the situation remedied. People don't step on each other's pride intentionally unless they are certifiably cruel. Communication is prevention.

LAW 7: A Job Can Only Be as Successful as the Means Supplied to Measure It

Business Executive. Almost every planned action in a business environment is objective and thus measurable in one way or another. Records are kept for an unforgiving government; reports are written by a careful staff. There is no reason for having a vague measurement on a specific job unless those involved want it to be so or are uninformed. It is much to the advantage of the BE to make certain that measurements are determined right up front.

Family Executive.   Almost everything that happens in a family environment is subjective or emotional and not too measurable. Grades, allowances, budgets, and such are specific, but privileges, diets, household tasks, and the like are not. It is to the advantage of the FE to make certain that measurements are routinely discussed when each task is allocated. At least everyone should agree on when the job can be considered complete.

Comment.   Both executives need some sort of measurement on the tasks they delegate, as well as some for their own work. The BE again has the advantage because so many records are kept anyway and fellow employees have been trained to utilize them.

The FE has a big problem with this, because very few records are kept and the family has not been trained to work that way. But measurement up front is a vital part of the prevention scheme. Peace in the family is a function of eliminating argument by agreeing on standards before the fact.

LAW 8: People Are More Important to Situations than Things

Business Executive.   It should be clear to today's BE that people produce company income more than machines do. Unfortunately, the productivity measurements are oriented toward production of hardware by machines. But the majority of workers are involved in white-collar tasks, service, word processing, and so forth. When a computer maintenance service person costs you $85 an hour from the company that sold you the machine, you figure there is more money in service than in manufacturing.

Therefore, the up-to-date BE concentrates on upgrading the competence of the people rather than machines. Marketing workshops are replacing machine-shop seminars. Personal computers are replacing the supersized ones. If all of this sounds as if it might be coming undone, you might be right. People make things, and we mustn't forget to encourage them to continue, or there will be nothing to service.

Family Executive.   A family has no required number of things the way a factory does. A family doesn't even need a home to be called a family although most of them manage to live together somewhere. But families traditionally spend more time with things than they do with each other. Yet, they all know that the greatest warmth comes from personal contact, not from a stereo.

The FE has to establish a program so that it becomes a primary concern of family members to know how the people are and what they are working on at that moment.

Comment. Many companies expend a lot of sincere effort in trying to establish their organization as a "family," and some have had good success. However, the feeling usually diminishes rapidly when the originator leaves the scene. Real families grow stronger and come together more when the leaders depart.

LAW 9: Improvement Is the Only Practical Management Goal

Business Executive. The world of business is a world of numbers and charts. Everything is measured in some way or other. The accountants, quality control people, inventory and traffic specialists have thick reports waiting for their chance to be shown.

In case the BE can't think of what to measure, the business magazines provide a constant stream of helpful ideas and show how the competition is working to measure what wasn't considered previously measurable.

So if you are interested in providing a goal that will make you look good as a BE, you can select any of these charts or reports and vow to decrease costs, increase profits, reduce turnover, eliminate waste, or any one of hundreds of worthwhile activities.

The opportunities for improvement are everywhere because the whole system of business management is based on numerical systems of varying degrees of sophistication. No matter how clumsy the system, there is still something that can be identified for improvement. That is the only thing upper management likes to hear.

Family Executive. The world of the family is a wasteland when it comes to numerical measurements. Outside of the kid's report cards or the breadwinner's paycheck, there is little to report on a formal basis. Miles per gallon, butter per week, haircuts per year, and other subjects are significant but are remembered, not necessarily documented.

Yet the FE has a big responsibility to keep the family oriented toward improvement in a methodical fashion. The subject of visible measurement must be introduced early in the formation of the family. Then it will become a part of the scene. Once the charts are around or the measurement format is in existence, family members can be helped to set improvement goals.

Weight charts, household duties, savings programs, educational activities, sports participation, time it takes to walk home from school—all of these and more. The whole idea is to get people in the habit of thinking that measurements are made to be improved upon.

As this is made part of the lifestyle, there will be fewer negative thoughts. After all, who would be interested in "divorces per person" or "colds caught each year" or "splinters driven into feet" or "classes failed" as objectives? The way to keep people on the improvement trend is to help them get in the habit. Then when they go to work, they will automatically be recognized as a comer.

Comment. The overall goal should always be to improve. It is not, however, necessary to set specific goals that can always be met. Easy goals make lackadaisical participants. I know that even a humble golfer such as I plays much better on a difficult course. I seem to go to sleep on the easy ones and find myself in constant difficulty. Concentration is the result of constant attention to improvement.

LAW 10: Nobody Really Listens

Business Executive. I don't ever remember a course on listening being offered as part of any management development program. It may be that listening isn't all that teachable, or it may be that most people think they are great listeners. Somehow, all the instruction I had was limited to the firm suggestion that a good listener is well respected.

Unfortunately, listening is really a matter of critical importance in the business world. Understanding cannot be obtained from simply reading or speaking. Others have to be able to communicate with you.

For the business executive, the problem is getting others to listen to the ideas and propositions and plans the BE wants to put forth. There is an entire industry for preparing slides, charts, presentations, and other devices to increase the probability that someone will absorb the BE's message. The advertising world works day and night to reach us; their success varies enough to show that it is not an exact program. One never knows exactly what will or won't work.

The best advice I can provide for the BE on this subject is first, find something to say that is worth hearing; second, say it within 3 minutes.

When teaching Quality Management, I always teach my students to learn an "elevator speech." This is the all-encompassing, action-producing set of ideas and actions that you pronounce while on the elevator with the big boss for just 1 minute. Your big chance to be heard can pass you by if you are not prepared to be listened to.

Family Executive.   To try to tell your children what the world is going to do to them if they don't follow your advice is a way to drive yourself insane while accomplishing nothing. Even if they'd listen, they probably would not act on what you said.

I propose that this fact be recognized and that the better approach is to establish jointly agreed-upon rules of performance—in writing—and then offer to answer questions, not offer advice. If "advice given only when asked" is the rule, you may find them highly agreeable to listening.

Comment.   In business, people will usually make an attempt to look as if they were listening anyway. In the family, little effort is made to pretend. At least you know where you stand.

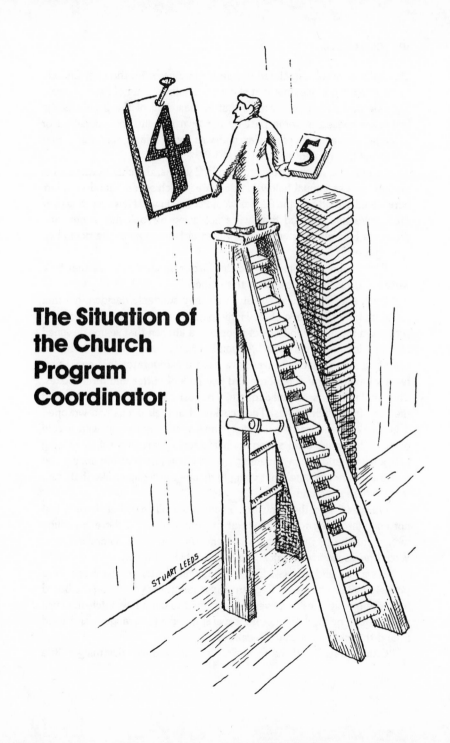

The Situation of the Church Program Coordinator

STUART LEEDS

Ellie Adams, newly appointed program coordinator for the First Church, found herself in a dilemma that she was certain was not of her own making. She had become convinced that at least half of the problems she had were caused in some part by her own inability to understand or manage. However, a particular one was very clearly something over which she had no control.

In a nutshell, it came down to this: In 2 weeks, the church was scheduled to have its annual fellowship dinner at which several hundred members would attend and the Circles would cook dinner. However, this year the Circles had decided they were not going to cook the dinner, and therefore Ellie was left with the problem of feeding all of the people on a budget of $100.

"Why," said the minister "did the Circles suddenly decide that they were not going to participate in this dinner?"

"Well, Joe," said Ellie, "it isn't that they suddenly decided. It's that for some time they have all been complaining about how difficult it is to prepare a meal for hundreds of people in a kitchen that seems designed for some intimate apartment. As you know, we have only one oven, we have two heating elements, and we have a refrigerator that could perhaps take one large milk bottle and two pats of butter and three Cokes. The whole thing is just inadequate. The last two times people trucked the food from their homes. They cooked it in their ovens and wrapped it in blankets and dashed it down, and we still wound up with a cold dinner. They have been asking the board for 5 years to consider redoing that kitchen, and the last meeting minutes you just sent me announced that they were absolutely not going to do one more dinner like that. And that's where we stand."

"Oh, yes," said the minister, "I remember all that, but there is just not enough money for a kitchen at this moment. Or if there is enough money for the kitchen, there's not enough money for something else. Well, I guess we are just going to have to think of a way around this."

"A way around it?" said Ellie. "What kind of way around it can there possibly be? I'm not going to go through the business of asking the board for more money. Besides, even if we wanted to get a new kitchen, which we certainly need, it would take several months to arrange it and build it, and the meeting is only 2 weeks off."

"Okay, okay," said the minister, "let's think about this thing a little bit. Why don't we have a meeting of the fellowship committee this evening and see what we can arrange? In the meantime, let's sit down and have a quiet prayer about it, and maybe we'll get some sort of message."

That evening the fellowship committee gathered in the minister's study, and as the members were filled in on the details, they began to squirm and wiggle. It was obvious that the only solution that came immediately to mind was to cancel the fellowship dinner, which had been a very popular item on the church's agenda.

"It's obvious to me," said Carol Thompson, the head of the committee, "that one thing we cannot do is consider canceling the meeting. Somehow or other, we have to get our act together on this."

"Well, I agree with you," said another member. "Let me suggest that we consider some of the Situation Management alternatives here. What is really our main problem? Our main problem is that we don't have the facilities for preparing food here. And we don't have the Circles, who usually prepared it at home and brought it in. They've gone on strike, so we can't use them.

The minister said, "Hmmmmmmm, are you suggesting that we find another source of the food?"

"That seems reasonable to me," said the other member. "We could have it catered."

"I checked into that," said Ellie, "and the minimum we could get away with would be $8 a head, and that wouldn't be much of a meal. If you figure 300 people, that's $2400. That gives me a $2300 problem, because I've got $100."

"What could you get," asked Carol "for $100?"

"Well, for $100 we could get enough cooked sliced beef from the butcher down there to feed 350 people—if they didn't eat too much. That's really like one and a half slices apiece. Or we could get enough sliced ham or sliced turkey to feed about 400."

"That's interesting," said Carol. "Let me see now, what's the biggest crowd we ever had?"

"Last year," said Ellie, "we had 175. This year we have reason to believe we'll have 200."

"Okay. So now, what did we want to have for dinner? We wanted to have some sort of meat, a salad, a vegetable, and dessert."

"Right, and we'll also need something to drink. But we have a couple of coffee pots and we can prepare coffee and bring in a punch . . . Maybe we can get the junior high Sunday school class to make up a punch."

"What are you thinking?" asked the minister.

"Well," said Carol, "what I was thinking is if we could get all of the people who are coming to bring something, then we would have enough food. It's either have them bring something or charge admission, and it doesn't really seem right to charge admission for a church fellowship dinner."

"Hey, wait a minute," Ellie said. "I think maybe you've got an idea there. We could have everybody bring their favorite dish, and then we'd all have enough." "Never work," said the minister. "Everybody will bring a dessert, and we'll wind up with three tons of dessert and no salads or vegetables. We have to have a way of distributing it."

"Okay, a way of distributing it. What we can do," said the other member, "is divide it up by last names. People whose last name begins with the first third of the alphabet can bring a vegetable. The people whose names begin with the second third of the alphabet can bring a salad. And the people whose names begin with the last third of the alphabet can bring a dessert."

"Well," said a member of the committee, who was also a statistician, "I think that works out pretty well. But you can't go by thirds, because if I remember right, something like half of the people in the phone book are in the first third of the alphabet."

"Well, that's easy to solve, we'll just take the phone book and divide it into thirds. Whatever letters go with that, we'll work with."

"Terrific! Terrific!"

So Ellie was assigned to search out the letters, and the head of the fellowship committee wrote a letter to the congregation, saying that this was the way the fellowship dinner would be handled this year and perhaps in the future. And then all the committee members sat back and held their breath.

The night of the dinner, 350 people arrived bearing food. The meat was gone in the first half hour. Fortunately, the butcher, who was a member of the congregation, was able to dash back to his shop and put together a couple of trays of ham and turkey and beef and whatever else he had lying around. These he donated to the meeting because he was so delighted to see the turnout. The Circles were happy because they were relieved of their responsibility, although they were a little miffed, perhaps, because they hadn't thought of this idea. Ellie and the fellowship committee were ecstatic. As years went on, this practice was continued until it became a solidly entrenched tradition. What's more, the activity drew the greatest participation of any church event in the course of the year. In fact, it became necessary to divide the fellowship dinner into two sections until a larger assembly hall could be built.

If you look back on the way this sort of thing came to pass, you fall into the question of what is the purpose of the staff of an institution or an organization. For years it has been obvious to me that all institutions are run for the benefit of the staff. If you go to a hospital staff cafeteria and listen to the discussion that goes on between the nurses, orderlies, and doctors, you will find that very little of the discussion centers around the patients. I know that the people in soap operas on television talk about the patients, but in real life they talk about the management of the hospital, they discuss the benefits and obligations of the staff, and they gossip about the activities of different individuals.

In U.S. associations, of which there are something like 28,000, there's usually a professional staff to manage association matters. Very few of that staff's activities are centered around the actual business of the people who belong to the association. Their time is spent mostly on directing operations and figuring who's responsible for what and that sort of thing.

In this case Ellie and the staff of the church had fallen into the trap of assuming that all activities had to be conducted and planned by the staff and administered by special groups. The thought that the congregation as a whole could do something hadn't previously occurred to anybody. Yet the old "pot luck" dinner had been the stable activity of church groups for years and years. It wasn't until church groups got staffs at all that they started organizing things so that the congregation, all of the participants, didn't have to do something.

Another interesting thing happened to this particular church as the Sunday school started to grow and a shortage of teachers developed. The members of the religion education committee, meeting with Ellie and the minister, were tearing their hair and anguishing over the lack of trained instructors and teachers for the burgeoning school. And at that very moment they had no teacher for the entire fifth grade, and they lacked a teacher for one of the seventh, eighth, and ninth-grade classes and for two adult classes.

The minister said, "I have been thinking about this, and I have come to the conclusion that we get much too much involved with the business of trained teachers. You get to thinking, 'Where are these trained teachers going to come from and what constitutes a trained teacher?' The only people we have to rely on are new members who transfer from some other church where they previously taught Sunday school. I think we ought to rely more on our present congregation."

"What do you want to do?" asked Ellie. "You want to have a lottery and assign people to different classes?"

"Well, a lottery is not a bad idea, although that perhaps is not in keeping with the principles of the church. No, all that I was going to suggest is that we have available the material on how to teach each grade. We can assume that people who join the church in the first place are interested in some sort of education and growth and want to participate. I realize that not everybody is a born teacher, but I'm also not really sure exactly what it means to be a born teacher. I think teaching is mostly hard work, and I think the Sunday school staff should maybe conduct a little refresher class for teachers on the organization of the material and help them with class discipline."

"Okay," said Ellie, "so what do we do now?"

"Well," said the head of the religious education committee, "if this is what you've been led to, I suggest that we open the door of the room and sit here and look out into the hall. When the next member of the congregation goes by, we ask which of these classes that person would like to start teaching next Sunday." So the group opened the door, sat, and watched the hall.

John and Lisa Smith came by on their way to pick up their child from the nursery. As they passed the door, the minister called them in. After Ellie nervously outlined the proposition to them, Lisa Smith said, "Why I think that's a terrific idea. We would like to work with the seventh, eighth, and ninth graders in one of their classes. Perhaps it would help them since we're not very old, and we think that that would be good training for us as we try to learn to raise our children."

John said, "Well, I'll be willing to try. So what do we do now?"

"Well," said the minister, looking as though he had planned this thing for some time, "the religious education committee is going to offer a special instruction course for new teachers beginning next week. In the meantime, ..ere's the material that goes along with the course. We'll all participate with you in any way you want."

So they shook hands all around, John put the material under his arm, and off the couple went.

This approach was repeated until the committee had recruited all the teachers that were needed. (Only one member begged off for a while, since he had a heavy travel schedule.) And this approach became the practice for the church. Over the years, the Sunday school seemed to be just as good as anybody else's Sunday school, and there was no lack of teachers. One interesting thing was that the adult program which for years consisted of one poorly attended class taught by a very experienced teacher, suddenly blossomed into eight separate classes after a year's experience with this new approach. The attendance represented 70 percent of the adult membership of the church. Given some opportunity for success and reassurance, people will come through.

The family executive should consider this case in the light of family management because what it says is that the members of your family are usually ready for more responsibility and more active participation than you are ready to give them at any given moment. I think it is a good idea, for instance, when traveling with children to let them make some of the arrangements. Let them read the road map and tell you where the place is to turn and where it is not. Let them pay the bills in the restaurant and learn how to tip. Let them learn how to get the seat selections at the airport.

All of these things can be readily done by people 12 years of age and sometimes less than that. This type of experience not only adds to their information bank but is terrifically reassuring. Many times you see parents traveling with children and treating them as if they were completely uninformed and unintelligent. They yank them around and make them stand here and make them stand there. The children become troublesome not only because they feel they have no participation in what is going on, but because they feel that the parent feels that they are completely inadequate.

I have watched married couples traveling and have seen husbands who are so obsessed with the business of making arrangements that they completely exclude their wives from all of this. Every now and then, I see a wife doing it the other way around. Admittedly there is not enough to do in traveling to keep two people busy, and one should not be meddling in what the other is doing, but there is no reason that duties can't be shared. There is no great amount of participation and training involved in learning that what one person may want in a seat is: no bulkhead; no smoking; and no window.

The Situation of the Boss Versus Peace and Quiet

The big boss has just accused you of having an out-of-control situation in your department. You know this is not true. What do you do now? (This situation is to prepare you for the Situation Analysis format.)

You (Harriet Jennings) are the quality control manager in a large company. For you everything is coming up roses. There are no major nonconformance problems. Production is moving out the door on schedule. The customers are happy with the product, and the engineering department has just agreed to install a new drawing control system that will make your job even easier. All is well with your world. You have been firm but fair, and the company is far ahead of where it was when you arrived. Costs are down. Product quality is up. You are a happy person, Harriet Jennings.

As you stroll to the executive dining room, you turn a corner and there before you, with fire in his eyes, is the big boss. He sees you; he steps forward; he speaks: "Jennings, all I have been hearing about are the quality problems on the stuff we get from our suppliers. It seems to me that we shouldn't have these problems if your department is doing its job. I'd like to hear how you intend to fix this situation. Put it on the schedule for the staff meeting tomorrow."

Without waiting for an answer, he stomps off.

What are you going to do now, Harriet? Your bonus, your reputation, and possibly your job are in danger. (Law 1 rears.) You don't know of any big problems with suppliers. Or have they been lying to you? Should you:

1. Rush back to the office, call your people responsible for suppliers' quality, and read them the riot act? (They let you down.)

2. Dust off your air travel card and head for the major suppliers' plants to see what they have been up to? (This way you might be able to avoid the staff meeting.)

3. Gather all the supplier data you can find, pore over it with your staff, and then create a chart-filled presentation for the meeting to show that things are in better shape than they have ever been?

4. Resolve to go to the meeting without any preparation and sit calmly, accepting any blame that might come along and asking for suggestions for improvement? (You know this will take the wind out of their sails.)

The question is which, if any, of these courses should be followed. Perhaps you might choose variations of the several. Heaven knows there are an infinite number of ways for managers to place themselves in a box.

This veteran Situation Manager knows, however, that she must think before acting. This is particularly true when people who have a direct influence on career, reputation, prestige, or peace of mind are involved. Since that involves almost everyone, it becomes plain that things must be thought out.

So Harriet retires to a quiet spot and starts to ask herself some questions.

Q. Why am I so concerned?

A. The big boss is upset with me.

Q. Why is he upset?

A. Because the suppliers are out of control.

Q. Is that what he said?

A. No. He said, "All I have been hearing about are the quality problems on the stuff we get from our suppliers."

Q. You make out the official problem reports. You don't remember any big suppliers' problems. And besides, you haven't talked with the boss for a month. So where did he hear it?

A. Let's find out who he has been talking to.

What now, Harriet? Just in case, call the suppliers' quality people and ask them how things are going. "Never better," they reply. Further questioning produces no indication of trouble or loss of faith. There must be another source, and that source's information must be questionable, or perhaps yours is wrong.

First stop—purchasing department.

Cal Foster, the purchasing manager, is sitting quietly at his desk, trying to work his way through the "in" basket. He smiles as you come in, but does not appear overwhelmed with emotion at your visit. After bringing each other up to date on family health, vacation plans, and local gossip, you casually approach the subject of suppliers' problems.

To your surprise, Foster immediately plunges into a list of the virtues of your people who have been working with his buyers. Seems that things have never been running so smoothly, although he thinks you could speed things by a quicker receiving inspection.

The chief buyer sticks his head in the office at that moment and with little invitation immediately recites the same speech, including the part about speeding up receiving inspection. You resist the temptation to suggest that they order sooner, thank them in a polite manner, and proceed. They don't seem to have any problems that would warrant such an uprising by the old man. Perhaps we'd better give this another "think."

Q. Who would be affected by defective products from suppliers?

A. *a.* Purchasing—because it would cause them to miss their schedules in delivering to manufacturing.

b. Manufacturing—because it would delay their work or cause them some rework costs.

c. Sales—because late deliveries would provide them with a loss of face to the customers, and they always are overoptimistic anyway.

d. Customers—because if they found a defect that we hadn't caught, they'd blame us.

e. Finance—because the rework, warranty, and scrap costs would go up.

Q. Do you intend to spend your whole life on this situation? You've only got 24 hours before the meeting. What's a better approach?

A. I could find out where the big boss got his information.

Q. Great! All you have to do is ask him. How are you going to do that?

A. Without asking him.

Armed with this reasoning, you march down the hall to the deputy of your antagonist and explain that he has asked you to check some facts for him (true), but you are not sure of the source (true) and don't want to bother him (true). So, could she fill you in on his schedule for the past 2 or 3 days? Maybe then you could figure out who he has been spending his time with.

She knows you're in trouble, and you know she knows. However, she informs you that if you hadn't missed the previous staff meeting, you would have known that the big boss had spent the last 3 days at the annual sales meeting in Chicago and had just gotten back that morning.

"Whom did he travel with?" you ask, and she gives you the list. To nobody's surprise, it contains only the names of sales reps.

Bob Blanford, the sales manager, is happy to see you. After stressing the fact that you exist only to serve him, you pop the important questions: "How do you feel our supplier quality program is going? Do you know of any significant problems in that area?"

Does he? "Do you realize," he demands to know, "that we lost thirteen important sales on the Widget 5 line this quarter because our input feeder, made by Glick and Sons, doesn't have a reaction time fast enough for our customers? It's too slow by 30 percent. You guys have to get these people on the ball. If they can't make it right, then let's get someone else or make it ourselves."

He stands up and approaches the blackboard, chalk in hand, to give you the full lecture. Hastily you stop him to explain that the Glick and Sons unit works just like the requirements given them and that you doubt if the rest of the equipment could accept the information that fast anyway.

Blanford indicates that engineering gave him the same story, but that he has to sell what the customers want, and that perhaps we'd all better get with the state of the industry.

At this point we'll impose a little suspended animation in order to provide thinking time. Obviously this is the source that the big boss found for his information. Just as obviously, the problem does not lie with the supplier or your people. However, he is speaking the truth and something should be done. The question is: How do you get done what must be done and at the same time get yourself off the hook the boss has got you on without making a permanent enemy of the sales manager, Harriet?

After a prolonged discussion, you prevail on Blanford to invite the engineering manager to the meeting. The three of you plan an item for the staff meeting, and using your newfound influence with the boss's deputy, you manage to have it placed first on the agenda.

At the staff meeting, Blanford makes a brief presentation in which he states that, although the present product meets the current specifications in all respects, it is necessary to consider a redesign to speed up the system. He urges that engineering be authorized to proceed and that after new specifications have been developed, the same suppliers be asked to participate in creating the system since they have been doing such a fine job on the current product.

"Including Glick and Sons?" asks the big boss.

The sales manager stares at him in disbelief. "Certainly," he replies, "they are our most consistent supplier. High quality all the way."

The meeting continues and the supplier-quality item is never mentioned again.

Analysis

We have seen how our novice Situation Manager extricated herself from this problem. Even so, she did lose a little face and a few points by permitting the situation to occur at all. The sympathetic soul will now comment that this woman had little control over what the sales manager said to the boss; yet Harriet Jennings let herself in for this situation because she did not take steps to prevent it. It is apparent from the conversations with the purchasing and sales managers that she had not been taking time to find out what was on their minds. Thirteen sales were missed over a 3-month period—not in one day. The sales manager must have been concerned before he finally spilled all to the boss. Regular visits from Harriet would have turned this up. The problem's solution became apparent as soon as they had discussed it. That could have happened just as easily 2 months before.

Concerning the subject of supplier quality, you can bet that Harriet is headed for further trouble. She has not been communicating with purchasing and has been leaning on her people's reports excessively.

The most important aspect in preventing difficult situations is to establish a continuing relationship which encourages people to tell you the troubles they think they have with you, prior to telling others. If, by constant contact, you establish the relationship—and accept their problems in a positive manner—life will become easier.

The easiest way to train your fellow managers in this method is to make heroes of them every chance you get. Harriet let the sales manager be the hero in the case study, but the motives were geared to save her own neck. Not noble perhaps, but effective.

The ABCs of
Situation
Management

The types of situations that concern us involve only relationships with people. We will leave the resolution of physical danger or appliance-malfunction problems to the adventure stories. They are best solved by reflexes, prayer, resolve, or a good mechanic. People-relationship situations require only some thought, consideration, and a plan for resolution.

As we toured through a day in Harriet Jennings's life, it became apparent that she thought before she acted. That is the key point in the entire exercise. A situation worthy of our attention and concern is also worthy of a thoughtful evaluation. Therefore, we need a guide to make sure that all the facts are taken into account, since it is possible that we may become emotional enough to forget some important considerations.

The first step in Situation Management is to separate yourself from the situation environment and study the thing. It is not necessary to fly off to Mexico. An office, a parking lot, a park, or even a phone booth will do nicely. All you need is a place free from distraction for a few moments. The results will be even clearer if you can make yourself write the answers.

Separate your thinking into three areas and consider them one at a time: awareness, evaluation, and action.

Awareness

1. What seems to be the situation?
2. How did I find out that the situation existed?
3. What is the potential effect of this matter?
4. How serious is it? (If it is minor, determine whether it has possibilities of gaining importance and magnitude.)
5. How much time do I have to extricate myself?

Evaluation

1. What evidence leads me to believe that the situation exists?
2. What is the specific source of this evidence?
3. Do I know whether the evidence is factual? (If I don't know, how can I find out?)
4. Can I list the steps that created the situation? (Are any missing or vague?)

5. Whose mind must I change to resolve the problem?

6. What does that mind think now?

7. How will I know when the situation is resolved?

Action

1. Relate the key individuals to the key issues. (Try to boil this down to one sentence.)

2. Why do they believe this?

3. What would it require to separate them from this belief? (Without creating another situation?)

4. What is the best method to use in this separation?

5. How do I implement the method?

6. Once it is over, what steps do I take to ensure that it will never happen again?

If you ask yourself these questions and listen carefully to the answers, you will have a good chance of resolving the situation in an orderly manner. However, you must be sure that you have the whole story, not just part of it, and you must be honest with yourself. (Watch out for Law 6.)

If you don't ask the right questions, you don't get the right answers. Let's examine our questions more closely to make sure we will use them properly.

Awareness

1. What seems to be the situation?

We are all familiar with the situation comedy shows on radio and TV. They all essentially follow the same format. First, a set of circumstances is described (the boss is being brought home to dinner); complications arise (unexpected house guests—usually unrefined); then, the action takes place (keeping everyone apart by feeding one group in the kitchen and one in the dining room—this causes the host and hostess to eat two meals at once); next, the confrontation (when everyone discovers everyone else and someone is insulted— bedlam reigns); and finally, a solution is produced and all is calm again.

Real-life plays are not too different from the above scenario. However, the situation is not exposed to you by a clever playwright; you must describe and identify it yourself. You are probably the only person who knows enough about it to do so. Therefore, you might use one paragraph to answer this first question of awareness:

- I'm supposed to be at my son's graduation and at a business meeting in Miami on the same date. My family will kill me if I miss graduation. My associates will ruin me if I don't make that meeting.

- My headache is really bothering me, I don't remember anything after the El Chico Club last night, and where did I get that big dog that is tied to the bottom of the bed?

- At 3:00 P.M. tomorrow all the workers will line up for their pay, but our accounts receivable didn't come through this week. We have no money.

- Here I stand in the center of a strange town. I lost my wallet and don't even have a dime to make a collect call to the office.

- Where did I put that library book?

- In 15 minutes, 257 guests will arrive for the club meeting. The hotel forgot to take the steaks out of the freezer, so dinner will be late. The speaker got here early and is in the bar completely smashed.

2. How did I find out that the situation exists?

- You know that you are on bad terms when your lover refuses to answer the telephone and returns your letter, marked "Deceased."

- You begin to realize that a problem exists when the level of the water in the bottom of the boat is equal to the level of the water in the lake.

This type of situation is apparent to even the most indifferent observer. The more complex the situation, the less apparent it may be. That is why it is important to ask yourself how you found out the situation existed.

Did someone tell you? Did you smell it out yourself? When did you begin to have an inkling?

Harriet Jennings was lucky; she was told directly and firmly that she had a problem. She got the message quickly. Most times you just become aware that things aren't going right.

You're beginning to get looks from people, looks that are not common to your everyday experience. You begin to feel like the people in the bad breath commercial.

Consider the ancient premise that "the spouse is always the last one to know." There is only one reason for that. Everyone assumes that the spouse already knows and doesn't care. So they don't tell him or her. The same is true in managerial life. The one involved may be the last to know.

If the husband or wife doesn't find out when only three people (minimum) are involved, it is not too amazing. When hundreds of people may be involved, a manager like Harriet Jennings may suddenly find the walls coming down about her ears.

Therefore, it is important to the final solution to be able to state that your awareness of the situation came from somewhere. Your answer might be: I felt it, asked around, and there it was; my secretary told me; the boss hinted at it until I figured it out; I learned it in a bar from a stranger; my wife told my barber, etc. It doesn't make any difference really—it just matters that you know *how* you learned it.

3. What is the potential effect of this matter?

To prepare for this question, you must consider what can happen if the situation is not resolved. Harriet decided that she might get fired, lose face, or possibly be downgraded. It may be that she was overreacting, but she did have that feeling.

As Situation Managers, we should look at the situation in terms of how long the problem will persist if we don't do something about it and how permanent the consequences will be.

Flagpole climbers have very little use for deodorants—they don't need them. Salespeople could be in deep trouble if they forget. Eccentric millionaires can get by without paying their bills— somewhere there is a sympathetic lawyer the creditors can reason with. Salaried employees, regardless of rank, must not overlook theirs—a poor credit reputation is frowned upon.

Each situation must be considered in the light of the person it affects. The surest test of potential effect is the amount of uncomfortableness that the situation generates for you. If you don't make it go away, you will become even more pained.

4. How serious is it?

Now, this is the heart of the matter. You must decide how much of your attention you are going to give it.

The ability to recognize the significance or insignificance of a situation is a main skill of a Situation Manager. It takes just as much time to resolve something that is inconsequential as it does to tackle a monster. You must now decide.

Incidentally, in this matter of time, many managers say that they can't spare the time to think out and resolve situations because they have other things to do. I'd like to point out that those other things to do are unrecognized situations that will continue until given the proper attention. For instance:

"I have 23 hours of scheduled meetings a week." Who scheduled them? Who attends when you are on a trip? More than likely, the meetings are on different subjects but with the same people. The situation here is serious—management is out of control. It needs a little agenda organization.

"You can't get good people anymore. Have to stay on them all the time." Who selected and trained them? People work to the level they think you expect. If they feel that you think they aren't as reliable as their parents, they won't be.

"I'll just ride with it. Bosses change so quickly around here that it doesn't matter anyway." Maybe they're looking for the right person, one who can recognize and solve situations.

"It's always been that way." Probably will be until someone changes it.

"I just don't have time to think." Got time to put gas in the car?

So classify your situation as serious or minor, and treat it accordingly. If it is minor, move on to the next question. If you consider it serious, give thought to what it could develop into.

5. How much time do I have to extricate myself?

This question may not be as simple as it sounds. Harriet had 24 hours. She knew that because the boss told her so. The rules had been set for her. However, your particular set of circumstances may be different. The finality point might be vague; it may not exist to your knowledge. The only guidance I can provide is:

a. You probably have more time than you think you have.

b. Nobody does anything until just before the deadline anyway.

Therefore, consider that it must be resolved immediately, and do so. Otherwise, you will put it off and will probably be faced with solving it in parallel with another situation. (No one ever believes this, but I felt that it should be said anyway.)

At this point, awareness should be complete. You have decided that a genuine situation exists, that you are involved, and that it is serious or has the potential for becoming serious in terms of disturbing your orderly life, and you know how much time you have to get out of it. Now let's start breaking it down into manageable segments.

Evaluation

1. What evidence leads me to believe that the situation exists?

This may seem redundant, since we have already talked about how we discovered the situation. However, the awareness portion does not necessarily lead to the methodical listing of facts. We must make sure that we have evidence besides subjective or emotional deductions. Surely no one must feel more foolish than the suspicious husband who bursts into his wife's parlor only to find her drinking tea with his mother. He may have been outsmarted; however, it will be some time before anyone takes his suspicions seriously again.

The usual evidence that a situation exists is that other people think it exists. The more they tell you about it or discuss it, the more you are inclined to believe it. But to avoid the twentieth-century equivalent of "cry wolf," it is wise to document the main criteria in a short listing.

2. What is the specific source of this evidence?

There comes a time when you must present the facts to the jury. In this case the jury is you, and you are inclined to be sympathetic with yourself. However, this evaluation process exists only so that you can see if it is necessary to take action. Therefore, you must answer the question specifically and precisely.

The value in identifying the source, of course, is to evaluate the factual weight of the case by measuring your confidence in that person's integrity.

3. Do I know whether the evidence is factual?

Assuming that you have now decided that the source is an honest one, we must recognize that even honest people can be mistaken (Law 3). That is why legal systems develop courts of appeal, whether people want them or not.

If any doubt exists, it is necessary to create a test. Harriet probed the organization until she got a reaction. Separate fact from fiction before mounting your charger.

4. Can I list the steps that created the situation?

Harriet put together a train of events. From her preliminary investigation, she determined that the boss had spent some time with the sales manager following a disquieting session with customers. She could reconstruct the conversation that generated the statement about the big problem with supplier hardware. She could recognize that she had become the patsy. She could also recognize that everyone involved genuinely believed that she really was at fault.

However, if you cannot do this, if you find yourself glossing over spots in the story, then you'd better regroup and start over. Stories can be made to come out the way you want them to just by manipulating the evidence. But that is fooling yourself.

5. Whose mind must I change to resolve the problem?

We have already discussed the idea that situations only involve people and their opinions. Whose mind has to be changed? In many cases, several minds may require alteration; however, if you can start a chain reaction, the job becomes easier.

6. What does that mind think now?

Careful. Don't credit that mind with having all the information you possess. What does it *really* think? That you robbed a bank? That you were indiscreet? That you have been ignoring your responsibilities to play the horses? That you don't care?

Don't flail away at symptoms. Get to the meat.

7. How will I know when the situation is resolved?

Your reward may be having the key to the executive washroom returned to you, or it may be an absence of rancor or attention.

But you must establish a measurement that will let you know when you have reached the end of the trail. You must know when you are done. Preferably that end should have a number in it or a prescribed statement. Samples of these might be:

> *"John, there'll be a $1000 bonus for you next month."*
> *"Ellen, I was wrong on this item."*
> *"You're right, George, it is 37 inches."*
> *"Next time you people should check with Albert before you start talking about these things."*
> *"How do you feel we should handle this in the future?"*
> *"If all our operations were in this good shape, we'd have no problems."*

Action

Evaluation is over. Now it is time to become a person of action. What are we going to do about the situation? First, we must put the data in an action format. Let's see what Harriet did.

1. Relate the key individuals to the key issues.

"The boss thinks our supplier control is bad, and he got that impression from the sales manager."

2. Why does he believe this?

"He believes this because he knows he's got a problem, and poor supplier control is the first reasonable cause that has been suggested."

3. What would it require to separate him from this belief?

"It must be remembered that he is working on a problem that doesn't really exist; therefore, it cannot be solved. He must be made to know the real problem, so that we can act upon it. He must learn of this problem from the person who told him the wrong one. If this happens, we can move on the real problem and forget the false one."

4. What is the best method to use in this separation?

   "I must convince the source of the problem that he has not defined the situation correctly, get him to recant (while saving face), and let him provide constructive guidance for the company."

5. How do I implement the method?

   "I get the principals together and help them deduce what I have already figured out. Then together we present the plan."

6. Once it is over, what steps do I take to ensure that it will never happen again?

   "I will conduct regular meetings with my counterparts. If they have a problem, I will know of it first."

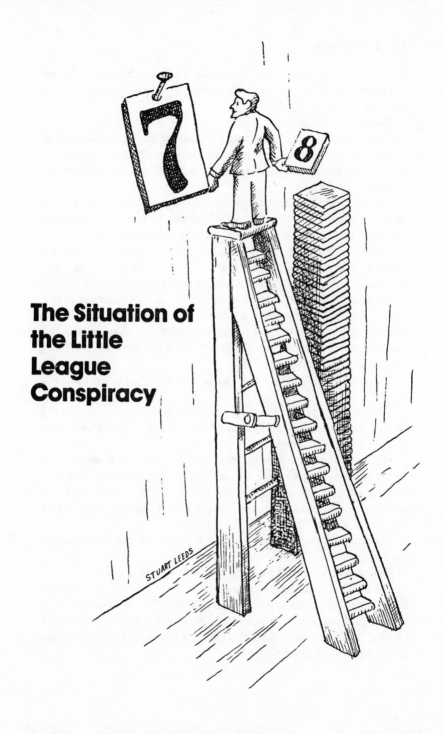

The Situation of the Little League Conspiracy

STUART LEEDS

Paul Phillips was accosted by his 9-year-old son with the directness usually seen in small boys. "Dad," he blurted, "you just have to take the job. You have to get involved."

"Involved in what?"

"You have to agree to become president of the Little League; otherwise, we won't have any teams and there won't be any games this year. Then I won't have any way to play baseball, and I'm just beginning to learn to hit the ball."

Paul calmed the youngster down long enough to find out that his teammates had heard their parents talking about how no one would take the job as president and that they would try to talk Paul into it.

"Never happen, son. There is no way they are going to get me into that thing. Sam Williams hasn't been the same since last season. Two years of it and the parents had him worn right down to the ground."

He pulled the boy to him and crouched so that they were eye to eye.

"Do you realize that being a Little League president can destroy a man? Do you really want your father to be out there raking grass, keeping score, building fences, explaining to mothers that their kids can't play every inning, and all that stuff?"

The boy thought about it and then looked his father in the eye as he said, "Yes."

When the delegation of managers and board members arrived to call on Paul that night, he quickly brushed them off and then served drinks to show he wasn't all bad.

"We're really not asking so much, Paul," said Hal Fenster. "The league requires that we have a president. Most of the volunteers want to be managers or coaches. We have lots of strong committees. There wouldn't be anything for you to do except to go to an area council meeting once in a while."

"And hand the mayor the first ball to be thrown out," volunteered another member.

Paul stood up and walked back and forth for a few moments.

"Ladies and gentlemen, let me give it to you straight. I won't go into my business obligations and my travel schedule. You all have that problem. And I'm not going to tell you that I'm not interested in Little League baseball, because I am. I think it is good for the kids. No, I'm not going to talk about all of those things."

"You already did," mentioned Sally Simmons.

Paul ignored the comment.

"What I am going to talk about is what I have seen while watching your last three presidents, none of whom are here tonight. I can only assume that they haven't been released from the rest home yet."

"Now that's not fair, Paul," said Sally. "We all work hard on this thing."

"I agree you all work hard, but you work hard on the games. The problems I am talking about are handling the equipment, collecting the money, preparing the fields, getting the sponsors, issuing uniforms, and all the things that I have seen the presidents do single-handedly. I tell you that if I were president, I wouldn't do a damn thing. Then if something didn't happen that some committee was supposed to do, I wouldn't run around fixing it. There just wouldn't be any game."

They all stood up and in one voice said: "Sold."

"What do you mean—sold?" gasped Paul.

Sally stepped forward.

"We are willing to meet your conditions. The board has agreed in advance to name you president and accept whatever conditions you name. Thank you, Paul. The kids appreciate it and so do we. The first full meeting is scheduled for next Wednesday at 7:30 P.M. in the school gym. I'll see you there."

And they disappeared.

The bedroom door was locked when Paul went down the hall.

"Let me in. What's the matter with you?" he shouted.

"You don't get in here until you get yourself out of that deal you just got yourself into," his wife cried. "I won't be able to go to the shopping center or anywhere without every mother in the area coming up to tell me how you are not treating her child fairly."

She finally relented, but the atmosphere was quite cool.

Paul worried about his commitment and how it would interfere with other projects he wanted to accomplish. Physical labor was not his thing, nor was being a one-man administration. Yet he had to admit that, although people and their kids only got involved for the fun of baseball itself, there were a number of talented and dedicated people involved. Perhaps they would do their jobs if they had the proper reminder and motivation. Or would they?

Before getting an ulcer, he decided to take out a copy of the Situation Analysis Guide to determine whether he could come up with an escape route.

SITUATION ANALYSIS GUIDE

Awareness

1.   What seems to be the situation?   I have accepted a job as president in an organization where the president traditionally does all the administrative and side jobs, in addition to being the whipping post for hundreds of emotional parents.

2.   How did I find out that the situation exists?
I have watched the people who held this job over the years rushing around, taking verbal abuse, and generally not enjoying themselves.

3.   What is the potential effect of this matter?
It could worry me and cause me to lose some effectiveness. If I suffer what the others have suffered, my wife will make life tough for me. If I cop out, my son will be disappointed in me.

4. How serious is it? The meeting is 2 days from now, and I don't have a plan. If I don't come up with a plan, I'm dead.

5. How much time do I have to extricate myself?
Two days.

Evaluation

1. What evidence leads me to believe that the situation exists? Personal observation of my predecessors and the general knowledge that people aren't exactly campaigning for the job. If it is so easy and uncomplicated, how come one of the others doesn't take it?

2. What is the specific source of this evidence?
The committee said that they had been trying for some time to find a president and that if I didn't take it, the kids wouldn't be able to play.

3. Do I know whether the evidence is factual?
I have witnessed all these things. In fact I even chewed poor Sam Williams out last year because I thought my son's manager was discriminating against him. I hope I am forgiven someday.

4. Can I list the steps that created the situation?
Over the years the administrative jobs have been

casually treated compared to the game itself.

Thus the persons who were president assumed the

tasks in order to ensure their completion. After

a while it was a fact of life that the president's

job included all the administrative work.

5. Whose mind must I change to resolve the problem?
The heads of the committees, the managers, the

coaches, and the parents. No problem with the

kids. They just want to play ball.

6. What does that mind think now?   They think that

the president is responsible for tending to all

the administrative details.

7. How will I know when the situation is resolved?
When we have had a successful year and I have not

done one lick of physical work; when all the com-

mittees are functioning as they should; and when

no parents contact me and give me a hard time.

Action

1. Relate the key individuals to the key issues.
Everyone involved in this league expects the president to do all the work.

2. Why do they believe this? All the previous presidents have always done all the work.

3. What would it require to separate them from this belief? To have a president that didn't work and to see that everything still got done, maybe better than before.

4. What is the best method to use in this separation?
Get the committees and other officials so involved that they will do their assigned tasks willingly. They have to make a commitment and believe in it.

5. How do I implement the method? I have to make myself a solemn promise not to follow up on anyone. Then I have to tell them all the way it is going to be, get them to agree, and keep it that way.

> **6. Once it is over, what steps do I take to ensure that it will never happen again?** If I handle it right,
>
> people will be fighting to be president of the
>
> league and bask in all the honor without doing any
>
> of the work. Then I will not have to do it again.

Paul reviewed the results of his analysis. It had become clear to him that the heads of the committees were the key. He had to really turn them on and keep them functioning during the season. How could he do that?

A review of the Laws of Situation Management might provide some insight into that problem.

"Funny," he thought to himself, "I thought these things only applied to business, but I guess all you need are people." He pulled out a clean sheet of paper and started writing his plan.

"Law 2 says, Loyalty is a function of feeling appreciated. That applies here. All I have to do is make sure that the appreciation comes from me. I'll provide some sort of visible recognition for the officers and the people who chair the committees. Everyone in baseball wears hats except the front office. We'll get them special baseball caps so that people will know who they are, and we'll recognize their efforts as they occur.

"Law 4 says, The effectiveness of any program depends on the amount of participation delegated. All I have to do is make sure that all the jobs are passed around and that everyone knows what his or her personal part is all about.

"Law 6 says, Pride goes before all. I'll threaten them with public exposure if they goof up.

"According to Law 7, you have to have measurement. These jobs are all ends in themselves. The equipment is either brought to the game or it isn't. The ball field is either ready or isn't. Either we have sponsors or we don't. That part should be easy.

"Law 9 says, Improvement is the only practical management goal. We'll have a bigger and better year than ever before.

"Law 10 says, Nobody really listens. This means that they will accept my plan at the meeting, but they won't think I really mean it. I'll have to make examples of some of them to really prove my point. That goes back to Law 6."

At the Wednesday meeting, Paul led the discussion of the various committees' tasks. The vice president would be responsible for the managers and umpires. There were committees for parent relations, grounds keeping, equipment, statistics, sponsors, awards, and player development. Each committee's specific functions were documented, and dates were set for task completion. Paul explained that the detailed duties of the committees would be printed and sent to each parent and player so that they would know who was responsible for what. He also made the point several times that if the committee didn't do the job, it was not going to get done. Everyone would know about it.

The head of the parent relations committee asked: "What do I do when a father tells me that his daughter only got to play two innings and the manager's son got to play all seven?"

"Tell him," said Paul, "to come on over to coach a team and then he can play his girl all he wants."

At the end of the meeting, Paul presented the special baseball caps. They were bright yellow because he wanted them to be seen. Everyone seemed pleased, and the meeting broke up in good spirits.

During the next 2 weeks, the functions of drafting players, getting sponsors, buying equipment, and so forth, went off with relatively few hitches. Everything was on schedule, and Paul was beginning to feel as if he had it made. He made a point of complimenting the committee members on their progress at the scheduled weekly meeting.

The day before the opening game, Paul walked across the field and noted that there were some holes in the outfield, that the pitching rubber had not yet been mounted, and that the base lines had been hastily made by pouring dry lime on the dirt. It obviously was not ready for the scheduled double-header to start the season. But he said nothing about it.

The next morning, as he escorted the mayor to the mound before the assembled players and parents, he noted that the field was still in the same shape.

Paul spoke briefly to the mayor who looked a little puzzled, then nodded, and moved off to the car. Paul picked up the megaphone provided for the official ceremony and addressed the quiet crowd.

"I am sorry to say that the game today will have to be canceled because the field is not properly prepared. It would be dangerous to play. The responsibility for preparing the field lies with the grounds committee." He stopped as a waving hand caught his eye. The grounds committee chairwoman, redfaced, was trying to signal Paul. Her eyes begged for mercy.

"However," Paul continued, "I am assured that it will be ready for the second scheduled game which will start at 3:00 P.M. The mayor will be back at that time and will throw out two balls just to make sure."

He never had any more problems.

The Situation of the Old Man and the Idea

STUART LEEDS

You're visiting a branch office. The manager is a respected old-timer with the company. He's also the president's brother-in-law. He's con vinced that your pet project is a bunch of baloney. If you don't sell him, it may well turn out to be just that. What do you do now?

When Alfred Tanner joined the Upperson Company, he immediately recognized that their internal communications system was decrepit, slow, and of course terribly inefficient. Every week, salespeople mailed their orders into a regional office where they were carefully sorted, classified, retyped, and sent on to the headquarters manufacturing office. After processing, the orders were distributed to a regional plant, where they were filled.

As a result, it sometimes took 6 weeks for an order to reach the manufacturing line. Customers would call a plant to find out what happened to their order before the plant even knew the order had been placed. Often the bills, mailed from the area office, reached the customer before the order reached the plant.

However, since the Upperson product was a unique and inexpensive thermoswitch, the customers had to be patient. No other switch could match its cost, reliability, and zero maintenance. Buyers were patient but not happy.

Tanner sized this up immediately. He set about developing a communications system that permitted salespeople to Telex their orders directly to headquarters in a format that could be instantly routed to the appropriate plant. This process would eliminate classification activities at the branch offices and permit those offices to concentrate on supervising the salespeople. A great many jobs could be eliminated, but since the company was shorthanded in other areas, the people could be used to fill open requisitions. All in all, it looked like a brilliant solution.

The president liked it. He was enthusiastic, so enthusiastic in fact that he gave Alfred an on-the-spot raise. Buoyed by this event, Alfred hardly noticed that he was being directed to prove the system in the field before incorporating it companywide. It was suggested that he start with the Atlanta manager.

Al was halfway through lunch with the Atlanta manager, George Webster, before he began to sense that he was in trouble. The older man had met him at the airport, hustled him to the car, and driven him a pleasant 15 miles to the country club. "A little lunch, a fast nine holes of golf, and a chance to get acquainted," George had said. "Always plenty of time for business, and it gets done faster and better when two fellows know each other."

The lunch and game were a delight to Al. George was one of the most knowledgeable and amusing persons he had met. By the time they were relaxing in the locker room, the day was almost over and not one word had been said about the new communications system. It was becoming apparent to Al that he was not going to get the opportunity to discuss it. Each mention of business brought from George short, amusing anecdotes on the philosophy of business, the point of each tale being that the young rush themselves to death and accomplish very little. Al decided to wait until the next day.

Upon reporting into the office the next morning, Al was hard put to get some time with George, who was continually tied up with customers and salespeople. He worked with Linda Pearson, the assistant manager, but soon ran out of things that could be done without agreement from George. Al began to realize that George was putting him off. It was apparent that George wanted no part of any kind of change, no matter how efficient it was supposed to be. He would particularly resist any change that did not originate from his own office. Frustration piled upon frustration as Al struggled to search out the required base data from the office personnel. They weren't going to help, at least not willingly. They would answer specific questions, but volunteered nothing. At one point, Al picked up the telephone to call headquarters and report the lack of cooperation. Then he realized that he would have nothing to report that would stand up. The assistant manager was at his service, and Webster really was tied up. The people were answering his questions. He had had a whole afternoon alone with the branch manager—what more could he want?

He was going to have to pluck this tough old bird himself.

That evening George Webster, Linda Pearson, and Al had dinner together. Al forced the conversation around to the new system. He stayed on it until George finally had to admit that he had, indeed, read the recommendations and did, indeed, consider them worthy. However, he could see no need for rushing into them at this time. Business was good, and the customers could be handled. After all, there had been many new people in the company with new ideas over the years, and "if we had done half of the things they wanted to, we'd be bankrupt now." George concluded his discussion with the recommendation that Al get a few more years under his belt in the company, and then they could discuss it some more.

Al pointed out the savings in money, time, and personnel. He noted that the company's controller had agreed that these savings would represent 8 percent of sales and would immediately produce an increase in profit. George wasn't impressed. The dinner broke up on this discordant note, but George did agree to give Al one uninterrupted hour in the morning to "try again."

A very disturbed young man wondered what to do. Why couldn't that idiot see the advantages to the company in this new method? Because it was new? Because it wasn't his? Because he really didn't think it would work? Because he didn't like him?

After some thought, Al decided that none of these things were the basic issue. There had to be something else, and he better find it quick. Now he knew why the president had picked this office to start. If he could sell Webster, he could sell anyone. If Webster didn't want to do it, the other managers wouldn't do it either. And for good reasons. George had always had the best-producing territory. He always met or exceeded his quota and groomed the executives of the company. He was riding right on top. Why should he go for a new scheme like this?

Alone that night in his hotel room, Al decided that he had come to the end of his road. All else having failed, he decided to try a little Situation Analysis.

SITUATION ANALYSIS GUIDE

Awareness

1. What seems to be the situation?   I can't convince Mr. Webster that my new system will be valuable to him. It doesn't turn him on.

2. How did I find out that the situation exists?
I have been listening to him, and there is abso—

lutely no indication that he is going to take it
seriously.

3. What is the potential effect of this matter?
Obviously, the system will not be installed if I
cannot overcome this objection. A person who cannot sell a perfectly good idea like this will not
be kept around very long.

4. How serious is it?   Very serious. It could cost
me my job, and it will certainly cost me a lot of
self-respect.

5. How much time do I have to extricate myself?
Not more than a few days.

Evaluation

**1. What evidence leads me to believe that the situation
exists?**   Personal observation and the spoken words
of George Webster.

2. What is the specific source of this evidence?
It is all around me. Nothing happens. No one is
interested.

3. Do I know whether the evidence is factual?
No doubt at all.

4. Can I list the steps that created the situation?
Yes, George is the "Duke of Atlanta." He has a

genuine success record in the company, and that

gives him a lot of freedom. He has no further

company ambitions and no fear. Therefore, he will

not do things he does not genuinely believe in.

5. Whose mind must I change to resolve the problem?
George Webster's.

6. What does that mind think now?   That this new

system will interrupt his orderly life and require

him to make changes that he didn't invent.

7. How will I know when the situation is resolved?
When the system is installed and working, and I

have George's support in putting it through the

rest of the company.

Action

1. Relate the key individuals to the key issues.
George doesn't want to put the program through

because he thinks it isn't going to do him any

good.

2. Why do they believe this? Because he doesn't

have any evidence that it is going to do him any

good.

3. What would it require to separate them from this belief? Show him how he could save a lot of time

that he could use for his own benefit, or show him

how he could gain something.

4. What is the best method to use in this separation?
Find out what interests him besides his job, and

convince him that he can do both better by using

this system.

5. How do I implement the method? First find the

other interest, then use salesmanship, and then

let him change the system enough so that he can

take some credit for it.

6. Once it is over, what steps do I take to ensure that it will never happen again? I'll make sure that people

> think they have a problem before I volunteer a
> _____
> solution.
> _____

After thinking the thing through, Al took a new tack with the older man. Instead of trying to sell his idea, he just listened. For 3 days he listened while George talked about the business, about himself, about the state of the country. Finances did not seem to be a problem to him, so Al discarded the thoughts of bonuses or rewards. George was already one of the top people in the company, and he had no desire to be president.

After much discussion and probing, Al finally found a clue—George was very interested in public service. George noted in passing that he had been asked to serve on the State Industrial Commission, an unpaid but vital job, and that he was really interested in public service. But he confided to Al that his job just didn't give him time to do it, and he did not feel that it would be fair to the company for him to take early retirement.

This, then, was the opening. Al pointed out that George could have his cake and eat it too if he could handle his job in less time. They made a rough analysis of how George spent his time, and found that two-thirds of his efforts were spent supervising the activities that would be eliminated under the new approach. Suddenly George became interested in the idea and, for the first time, examined it in detail. He pointed out several aspects to Al that required change or improvement, and the suddenly active Linda Pearson helped modify some of the transmission procedures to fit actual practice.

They outlined a seminar to be used in explaining the system to the sales reps and customers. George personally called all the other field managers and told them what a great thing this new system would be.

The system was installed over the next few months, and because of the support given by the field managers, it actually did work and actually did save the time and money that it was supposed to.

Al had learned an important lesson, but as he thought about it, he realized that he had learned it several years ago but had forgotten it. He leafed through his personal files and found an essay that had been written some time ago by a friend who was a value analysis specialist.

The chief executive of a company is approached by a corporate staff member with the suggestion that a certain amount of cost could be removed from the products by doing a value analysis engineering study.

Since there is no simple way out of the situation, the chief executive grants permission for the study and selects the product to be attacked. Unless he is an unusual person, he will probably pick the most difficult item in his line. The specialist accepts the challenge and goes to work.

Some time later the specialist completes the report and everyone is greatly pleased. Honest savings are shown to be possible through process changes, component substitution, work simplification, and other legitimate means. The changes are implemented. The study proves to be an unqualified success.

The chief executive is delighted, congratulates the staff specialist, and writes a letter of commendation to the corporation president extolling the extent of the accomplishment. The specialist returns to headquarters secure in the knowledge that there now exists a true believer.

Some time goes by and the busy specialist happens to think of that particular accomplishment. Why in the face of all that success, has there been no request for more help?

A call and a hint result in a polite brush-off. A personal interview reveals that the situation is exactly as it was before, except that people are, if possible, less interested. The activities are remembered as an interesting experiment, nothing else.

Producing a verified list of triumphs in other areas gains nothing except more inaction. The specialist returns home to think and ponder, a victim of "transient gratefulness." Why?

If you want to know "why," you must first remove yourself from the big picture and settle down to study the key person in the play: the division chief executive. What makes the CEO fail to realize the benefits of staff advice and effort? Advice and effort that are freely given and professional.

Well, the CEO doesn't really care about reducing the price of that item. Of course, it would be good to reduce the price, if possible, but that is not what this executive is working 16 hours a day for.

What the CEO wants is to be the leader in the field. There may be a desire to control the product market prices for the field. There may be all kinds of goals. But whatever the CEO wants, you can be sure that he or she knows it, and only he or she knows it.

Successful staff work can only happen when effort is guided along the path that will help that chief executive achieve personal goals.

Don't offer to help reduce product costs only because they can be reduced. Offer to help individuals meet their personal goals by helping them reduce costs or whatever it is you do.

Find out their goals—determine how your skills can help achieve them, and make your work commitment that way. It never fails.

Don't approach people with a solution until you know what their problem is. Your particular brand of happiness, remarkable though it may be, might not match theirs.

Anything can be sold to anyone if you can find the correct motivation. The unfortunate part is that the motivation usually has to originate with the person, and since individuals are apparently deep wells of complexity and unfulfillment, you may have to fish to find it.

Alfred Tanner went into this situation blindly and almost blew the whole thing. He was so sure of the worth of his plan that he neglected to evaluate its possible effect on other people. To him, the value was so obvious that he was a bit shocked not to receive the key to the city.

He found himself being successfully managed during his stay at the branch office. There seemed to be no way of escaping the friendly net that had skillfully been thrown about him. He was being smothered with cooperation and frustrated by the lack of commitment. He was a man with a solution who could not find the proper way to apply it.

This may occur to any of us, and when we recognize it, the time has come to regroup and plan a new approach. Lesser persons might have made reference to the fact that the corporate president wanted the program implemented. If that had been the case, the program probably would have been implemented, but would certainly have failed. "I knew it wouldn't work—and it didn't."

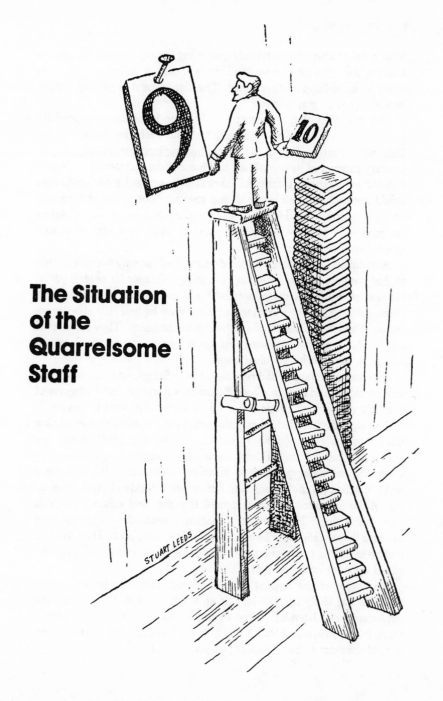

**The Situation
of the
Quarrelsome
Staff**

STUART LEEDS

Your subordinates are continually quarreling among themselves, and, as a result, you must participate in all levels of activity and problems. They seem to be drifting farther apart. The department is getting farther behind. What do you do now?

The manufacturing department of Fortune Industries contained 85 percent of the people and generated all the profit for the company. Essentially, Fortune was in the subcontracting business, having no proprietary product of its own. They had a complete metal-working operation and an extensive electronics fabrication business. Larger companies would contract out their small lot and specialty jobs to Fortune, usually on a short-term basis. However, the company had earned a reputation for good work and on-time delivery, so their customers kept them well stocked with orders.

Karl Jansen, the manufacturing director, had recently been promoted to that position, having served as purchasing manager for several years. He was pleased with the opportunity and quite happy that the entire manufacturing staff was staying with him, since he had little shop experience. The staff consisted of eight department heads. They supervised a total of 574 people and were considered by the company to be knowledgeable, hard-working professionals.

The manager Jansen had replaced, Harry Briggs, was now executive vice president and Jansen's boss. Sometimes Karl wondered why one of the eight department heads had not been moved up when Briggs left.

The eight departments of manufacturing were production control (Jim Baton); machine shop (Henry Rush); sheet metal shop (Al Bensen); electronics fabrication (Tim O'Rilley); electronics assembly (Kay Cross); manufacturing engineering (Lorraine Morano); maintenance (Dave Lyons); and inspection (Hugh Brown). Karl immediately decided to start an analysis of the operation to satisfy himself that the most efficient methods were being used. However, this analysis presented its own problem because there really wasn't anyone available to conduct it. The company had no industrial engineering or operations staff personnel who could be called upon for an evaluation of this magnitude.

Karl rejected the passing thought of asking his boss for assistance, since he was likely to consider this an indication that Karl thought the department had been left in bad shape. He considered calling in consultants, but observed that the company was not in the habit of using them. He did not want to be a pioneer just yet.

After reviewing the resources open to him, Karl decided to use his own managers in evaluating the department. What better analysis could there be than one conducted by the managers who ran the shops? He would assign them to teams, and each operation could be evaluated for the common good. His next staff meeting was scheduled for 2 weeks from that date, but having given birth to such a creative solution, he could not bear to wait. He called a meeting for the next day.

The managers were somewhat less than enthusiastic about the proposal. They realized that an analysis of this type should take place, but it was immediately apparent that each felt the need for improvement was in an area other than the one they ran.

In amplification of this feeling, they began to discuss the current requirements and oversights of the manufacturing section. Too many reports, too many meetings, and not enough corrective action by other management functions. They each had little trouble in their own area, but they were beset by inadequate material or services coming from the others. It was a rare demonstration, and Karl was a little terrified by the whole thing. They had been searching for a forum to obtain justice and looked to him to dispense it. He dismissed the meeting on the note that he would look into the situation and attempt to find a solution.

At home that night, Karl lifted the papers from his briefcase and paused for a moment to think of the meeting. Not a very good start. The managers felt no obligation to each other. They welcomed the evaluation idea only because it would, at long last, show the unfairness of the system thrust upon them.

He sighed and turned to the company mail he had not been able to read that day. Since there was a large stack, he separated it into groups. The groups became:

1. Company policy and procedure notices to be disseminated to his staff.

2. Memos from other departments concerning internal manufacturing operations.

3. Memos to him from his managers concerning problems in other departments and demanding solutions to situations that were interfering with their schedule.

4. Reports from the quality control department indicating that the defect rates were rising and corrective action was not being taken.

5. Memos from the sales department detailing customer dissatisfaction and stating concern with schedule fulfillment.

6. Rough drafts of reports written by his staff for his review and correction prior to issuance.

He struggled through the entire pile and disposed of all the documents. However, he realized that it was then well after midnight and that a similar stack would probably show up the next day. Something had to be done. Pouring a fresh cup of coffee, he sat back to review the situation. He must be doing something wrong. He decided to review the problem by utilizing the Situation Analysis Guide. Feeling a little silly, he picked up his pencil and began to fill out the form.

SITUATION ANALYSIS GUIDE

Awareness

1. What seems to be the situation? My staff is uncooperative with me and with each other. They do not seem to trust one another or have common objectives.

2. How did I find out that the situation exists?
I first became aware of it when I suggested a mutual efficiency analysis. Their reaction was very negative.

3. What is the potential effect of this matter?
If my department heads will not work together, I am doomed to failure in this job.

---

4. How serious is it?   Critical.

5. How much time do I have to extricate myself?

Usually a new department head has 3 months before

he is held responsible for everything that is

happening. I probably have 6 months, but I'll

concentrate on fixing it in 3.

Evaluation

**1. What evidence leads me to believe that the situation
exists?**   There are several symptoms: assignments

are routinely completed a little late; I must per-

sonally edit and revise reports; people are late

for meetings; administrative chores are always in

arrears; staff meetings are nonproductive; I am

involved with a half-dozen fire drills a day;

every problem is brought to me; we are behind

schedule and no one is to blame; and the managers

quarrel with each other.

2. What is the specific source of this evidence?

My own observations and the reports of the mea-

suring departments such as finance, quality con-

trol, and sales.

3. Do I know whether the evidence is factual?

Yes. I haven't verified each detail but the indication is overwhelming.

4. Can I list the steps that created the situation?

Yes, I think it was the result of management methods used during the years of building up the business. The shop managers never had much responsibility and top management was always available to them. The depth of this practice wasn't visible until now, when the business is too big for one person.

5. Whose mind must I change to resolve the problem?

There are eight minds involved--all of my department heads.

6. What does that mind think now?   Right now they think that their world begins and ends at the limits of their department. They feel no responsibility for the overall success of the entire operation.

7. How will I know when the situation is resolved?

When the operation is on schedule in all areas and

my staff is helping one another to resolve and

prevent their problems.

Action

1. Relate the key individuals to the key issues.
My managers think they are responsible for their

own departments exclusively and that they have no

part in the total operation, which they leave to

me. They are defensive and negative.

2. Why do they believe this?   They have been here
a long time and have not been asked to think

differently.

3. What would it require to separate them from this belief?   I think four things are necessary: (1)
I must establish better communications between

each of them and myself; (2) they need to have

better working relationships with one another; (3)

we need a mutually developed operations plan; and

(4) we require a measurement and problem action

system.

4. What is the best method to use in this separation?
Each item requires a different method.   For the

first one I'll set up individual meetings with them--a half hour each week. We'll stay away from problems and try to understand each other as individuals. Guess I'd better write a little sketch of each person, as I see them, in preparation for that. The second item requires them to learn to talk with each other. We can have better staff meetings and problem sessions, but after a month or so, I think we should all sit down and evaluate each other. Three and four should be a direct result of the first two. It would be dangerous to start them before the relationships are straight.

5. How do I implement the method? We'll start out slowly. I'll have a "What's your biggest problem?" meeting in the morning; then we'll start the individual and staff meetings. When they begin to show signs of being interested in each other's problems, we'll move on. Guess I'd better sketch out a schedule.

	Weeks											
	1	2	3	4	5	6	7	8	9	10	11	12
Daily "problem" sessions	x	x	x	x	x	x	x	x		x	x	x
Weekly individual sessions		x	x	x	x	x	x	x		x	x	x
Staff meetings	x	x	x	x	x	x	x	x	x	x	x	x
Weekly twenty-problem meeting			x	x	x	x	x	x		x	x	x
Self-evaluation				x		x				x		x
Group evaluation					x							x
Operations plan						x	x	x				
Measurement system							x	x	x			

6. Once it is over, what steps do I take to ensure that it will never happen again? I'm not sure about this, but I think if we are really communicating with each other, we will recognize changes as they begin to occur and will be able to alter our plan in order to meet them.

Early next morning, Karl called his managers together. He noticed that, as they straggled in late, each had a good excuse. However, he made no comment. After they were seated, Karl greeted them and began to speak:

"This will be a brief meeting. Its purpose is to get us started on a little different system of operating here in manufacturing. I believe that we need to get to know each other better and to know each other's problems. You are all experienced managers, so we should be able to develop a mutual assistance method. To do this we will establish three types of meetings in the department.

"Status meeting. Each morning at 8:15 we will meet for 15 minutes. I will ask each of you one question: 'What's your biggest problem?' You state that problem, and we'll go on to the next individual. We won't discuss the problems; we'll just state them. After the meeting you can get together with anyone whose problem is similar to the one you have or whose problem is one you feel you can help with.

"Staff meeting. Each Monday afternoon we will meet from 4:00 to 5:00 to discuss departmental operations and our nonproduct problems.

"Problem status. Each Wednesday afternoon we will meet from 4:00 to 5:00 to develop and discuss a twenty-problem list. I would like the chief inspector to maintain this list and to be responsible for that meeting.

"In addition, I would like to meet individually with you for a half hour every week, so that I can learn more about your operation and your people.

"Since we are all busy, and since we should set a good example for our people, it is imperative that each meeting start and end on time. I obtained a Salvation Army contribution can this morning and I'll put it on the bookcase. Anyone late for a meeting will contribute $1 to the can. If a meeting does not end on time, that will be my fault and then I will contribute. Any questions or discussion?"

Dave Lyons, the maintenance manager, nodded and said, "We already have a lot of meetings, Karl. I'm already scheduled for 22 hours a week. I hate to see us starting some more."

"That's a good point, Dave," said Karl. "I think one of the things we need to accomplish is to evaluate the meetings that occur in manufacturing and assess their purpose and effectiveness." He turned to Hugh Brown, "Hugh, let's make Dave's item number one on the twenty-problem list. Nothing is more important in this department than the time of the management talent."

No one had any more items, so Karl started the "biggest problem" session. Most of the staff had to pause and think about it. Lyons said "people." Karl wouldn't accept that; therefore, Lyons switched to "managers who don't tell me about equipment problems until the unit is a complete disaster." It took a few moments of confusion for Karl to remind everyone that the problems were only to be stated at this time and not discussed. They finally got through the meeting. As the department heads left, Karl noted that they were at least talking to each other, although there were few indications of warmth in the tones. Hugh Brown, who was the most senior of all the managers, was the last to leave. He paused for a moment at the office door and turned to glance at Karl, who was still sitting at his desk. Hugh nodded and gave Karl a slow wink before leaving.

The morning meetings had settled into an acceptable routine by the end of the week. The Salvation Army was $12 richer, and the problem statements were becoming more concise and pertinent. Karl noted that very few were repeated.

The staff meetings on Mondays went fairly well, although it was difficult to keep product problems out of the discussion. It was almost as difficult to get someone to accept action responsibility for an administrative assignment. Progress seemed slow to Karl, but he stuck to his schedule and, in the fourth week, began the twenty-problem meetings.

Everyone was interested in adding problems to the list, but less interested in accepting responsibility for resolving the problems in most cases. Therefore, Karl took the position of assigning each problem to two managers—the one whose area was most affected and the one whose area was least affected. That pleased no one, but it was some progress. At the second meeting, it was noted that no problems had been removed from the list and that several more were awaiting admission.

Karl reviewed his analysis again, gave himself a pep talk, and decided to enter the self-evaluation phase. His individual talks with the managers had produced some evidence that they, too, recognized the need to change the existing relationships. They were looking to Karl to accomplish it. Each knew, however, that it would require more than a directive to change people's work habits.

During his individual meetings the next week, Karl handed each manager nine slips of paper, explaining that they were identical forms to be used for self-evaluation. He asked the managers to complete one evaluation on themselves and then do one for each other manager, including him. They were to keep their own and place the others in a "personal and confidential" envelope until a special staff meeting which would be held the next Saturday morning at a local hotel. At that time, each person would be given the evaluations written by the other managers. Each could then compare these assessments with their own and determine where others had a different view.

Karl hastened to explain that no personal embarrassment would be involved since no one would see the evaluations but the person involved. They could ask each other questions about the evaluations if they wanted to.

The participants were not quite sure about this development, but they decided to go along with Karl, since there didn't really seem to be much choice. The form required ratings on ten different personal characteristics:

Name of Person Being Evaluated _____

Date _____

Characteristics	Rating		
	Poor	**Average**	**Very Good**
Cooperation with others	_____	_____	_____
Ability to listen	_____	_____	_____
Skill in expressing self	_____	_____	_____
Interest in helping others	_____	_____	_____
Communication with subordinates	_____	_____	_____
Ability to solve problems	_____	_____	_____
Ability to prevent problems	_____	_____	_____
Punctuality	_____	_____	_____
Ability to view objectively	_____	_____	_____
Stability of operation	_____	_____	_____

On Saturday morning, the nine arrived at the hotel. Following Karl's suggestion, they were dressed informally, but despite his urging, they were not very relaxed. After some coffee and shuffling around, they sat at the big table and started their session, Karl carefully choosing a seat other than the one at the head of the table. "I will be the chairman for this meeting," he said, "because I'm the only one familiar with the procedure. However, at future meetings we'll all vote on who chairs the meeting."

All the managers were asked to talk about themselves for 5 minutes, but with the restriction that no reference should be made to career— only personal activities such as hobbies, personal interests, birthplace, and so forth. Karl spoke first. By the time the third individual had spoken, the group relaxed and became interested in this other side of people they had known for so long. Lorraine Morano got so involved in talking about her hobby of raising roses that the chairman had to remind her of the time limits. Tim O'Rilley, they discovered, repaired old violins—but had never learned to play one.

When the last one had spoken, Karl passed out the completed evaluation slips. Each person received an envelope with eight evaluations completed by the other managers. In addition, there was a blank one. "If you take a few moments to summarize the totals and enter them on the blank copy, you'll have one form to deal with," said Karl. He went on to explain the rules of the meeting.

"You have each evaluated yourselves according to this format. Now you have this same evaluaion completed by those who work with you. The object of the session is to compare the two, noting the differences and then asking for comments on the items that concern you. For instance, I had rated myself as very good on 'ability to listen.' However, five of you rated me average and three poor. Obviously, we have different opinions. When my turn comes, I hope you will tell me frankly where you feel I am mistaken.

"We will start from one point around the table with one person who can ask questions to get the information. Then, we will move to the next, until everyone has had a turn. There are just three rules:

1. All comments must be constructive.

2. The questioners may not defend themselves.

3. The world is always present; reporters are not.

"Who wants to start?"

There was a brief silence; then Hugh Brown spoke up. "I'll be first, mainly because I seem to have run across a real conflict on two items. The first is cooperation with others. I always thought I went out of my way to be helpful. Anyone have any comments?"

Another silence.

Henry Rush cleared his throat. "Hugh, I think you're very helpful. In fact, the problem probably is that you're too helpful. I don't recall a discussion with you yet that you didn't eventually come around to my way of thinking about whether we could use some defective material or not. What I'm saying is that I think we have to look to inspection to be firm and make us do our job right. Sometimes you're too easy."

"But I have always felt that we should be reasonable."

"No defending," said Tim, smiling.

"Let me tell you the other item that bothered me," said Hugh. "I think it might have something to do with the first one, although it didn't occur to me before. That one is stablility of operation. I have had the feeling that my department is dependable and on time all the time."

"I think that's true, Hugh," remarked Kay. "Perhaps the reason you were rated low on that one is that you are not consistent in your standards."

Hugh looked puzzled. "How do you mean?"

"Well, I think an example would be best. I have just found out that some of my supervisors are saving parts that aren't quite right until the last of the month. They feel that inspection will accept them during that period, whereas they wouldn't touch them in the first part of the month."

"You mean that we're tough or loose, depending upon the shipping dates?"

"That's about it."

"Well I'll be darned. I think you're right. Let me ask about an item that I wasn't going to bring up because I felt that the ratings were absolutely wrong. That is ability to solve problems. I have always considered that my strong suit. May I have some comments on my low rating for solving problems?"

"I think, Hugh," said Dave Lyons, "that most of us are going to wind up with low marks in that category. I'm beginning to get the feeling that we have been solving the same problems for a long time without getting anywhere. That is because we have been working on the symptoms and blaming someone else for the situation. When my turn comes I want to get into that in detail. In your case, I have to say that your general approach is to resolve the problems that exist right now, not the ones that will affect tomorrow—only today."

Karl's turn was fourth, and by the time the discussion got to him, everyone was well into the spirit of the meeting. They really gave it to him on his tendency to brush aside excuses and reasons, but volunteered that perhaps they had not immediately fallen in with his action standards. The discussion became free and easy, and amazingly enough, each of them seemed to survive their turn without personal embarrassment or hurt feelings. They had picked up the constructive, friendly manner necessary in such activities.

At the end of the morning, Karl asked each person their opinion of the exercise. Their comments indicated that a good start had been made toward opening the channels of honest communication among themselves. A lot of the old barriers had been lifted, and they were aware of the need to be united in a common bond. Kay asked Karl what other things could be undertaken in order to further the process Karl tossed the question back at the group and was delighted to hear them decide to create a master operating plan for the manufacturing operation. They roughed out a schedule and agreed that the plan should be completed within the next 3 weeks. The first week was to be spent on a detailed evaluation of existing methods and a determination of weaknesses.

Over the next few months, the department gradually rounded into an efficient, on-schedule, problem-solving operation. The meetings became useful, problem lists were reduced, and a feeling of cooperation served as the basis for the entire activity. Karl was pleased with the result, but began to realize that he had made no provisions for preventing a recurrence.

This problem was presented to the staff. Their response was to establish a training program for the next level of management below them to ensure that the principles they were developing became part of the entire organization. In addition, they scheduled self-evaluation sessions with their subordinates.

It took some time for the managers to realize that the job of preventing a recurrence was a continuing one. But once it became routine, the task became easy. They decided to make out a 2-year operating plan and a 5-year operating plan each year. These would be reviewed in depth by all levels of departmental management, then presented to top management for approval. In that way, everyone would agree upon the rules of the game. Conformance to that plan established the basis for a measurement system that was fair and accurate. Raises and promotions would be given on the basis of meeting objectives, resourcefulness, and effectiveness.

The steps that Karl Jansen took to resolve his problem worked well for him. This does not mean that the same solution will apply to other operations. However, it does mean that by following the Situation Analysis Guide, it is possible to define a problem's basic elements.

Karl is a person after my own heart. He did not let the product problems cloud his judgment; he took the time to think the situation out. As a result, he put his finger directly on the basic problem: people relationships. Many managers would be tempted to blame everything on the staff and launch a campaign to whip them into line or replace them.

I'm sure we have all noted that some executives tend to collect a group of trustworthy managers and take them along to each new assignment or company. Certainly this has proved effective many times, but often enough it doesn't. An executive's reputation grows quicker and deeper when the material at hand is used to create success. Probably less than 4 percent of the business people in the world are unusual in terms of intellect and competence combined. These are the people who can identify problems, create solutions to fulfill the need, and implement the solutions while keeping everyone happy. There is no use looking for them through the Personnel Department; when they're ready to go to work for you they'll let you know. In the meantime, shape the tools on hand the way Karl did. Once the tools are sharp and working together, the other problems will be manageable.

We all live in a problem-oriented world. If we face this fact, it is only logical to consider the prevention and solution of problems as an authentic measurement of performance. However, we have to examine the specifics. Obviously, it is easy to measure the solutions of problems, yet it may be dangerous to assume that we know how to measure them until we have examined all the aspects of the problem. But it is easy to measure the prevention of problems without all the analysis.

This somewhat ambiguous-sounding statement has its origin in the fact that most managers are knowledgeable concerning any problem in their area of responsibility. It is impossible to tell the amount of actual effort being put forth on any particular problem by listening to the activity reports of the affected managers. Nor is it possible to determine the difficulty the problems present by observing the problem-reduction activity.

Therefore, we can only measure solutions by results: the problem is gone, forever and ever. It is only possible to measure prevention by the seriousness of future situations: good problem preventers only have minor problems.

By what standards should we measure a management team? They should be judged on the basis of their initial effort, their tradition of involvement, and their success in both preventing and resolving problems. The key points are these:

1. Susceptibility to problem eruption

2. Cause of typical problems

3. Seriousness of typical problems

4. Adeptness of problem identification

5. Skill in problem resolution

Let's examine the meaning and relevance of each point. If they are to be our key means of measurement, it is essential that we understand their content.

Susceptibility to Problem Eruption

What is the team batting average on problems in the past? Is this a group that always has problems that involve people outside their plant? Do staff experts spend a lot of time there? Are the recurring problems similar? Do they have the same problem several times as it flows through the plant?

Cause of Typical Problems

The cause I mean here is a differentiation between systematic problems and situational problems. Systematic problems arise because the operating program of the team did not permit heading off the problem or finding it early. This type of problem is easily identified because fixing or eliminating it forever means changing a procedure, a method of organization, or an operating plan.

Situational problems occur because something changes outside of the normal control of the team. It is possible to determine who is most responsible for the problems by categorizing situations according to organizational responsibility and being completely cruel about it.

Seriousness of Typical Problems

Problems that will vastly affect schedule, cost, or quality to a significant extent if not solved immediately are the type that show the management team to be delinquent in prevention areas. A successful team has only the small nuisance problems that occur from running a tight shop. These may lose some sleep for you, but will not put you out of business or lose you a valued customer.

The poor team always has "end-of-the-world" problems.

Adeptness of Problem Identification

The high-performance team finds its own problems, identifies them, and solves them. The high-performance team tells the customers and the corporate entity about the problems instead of vice versa. They have an accurate, dynamic, and topical reporting system that requires assessing the state of their activities on a daily basis. They cannot get too far into the soup without having a sign that something is changing. Planned detection is more important to success than unplanned.

Skill in Problem Resolution

How long does a problem stay resolved? How soon does it, or its brother, come back?

The Situation of the Unwanted Improvement

STUART LEEDS

Tom Johnson, a staff engineer assigned to the headquarters staff of XYZ Corporation, was called to his boss's office to discuss the Premier Pump situation. Tom had been in headquarters for only 3 months, having previously worked in the electronics system division for 6 years. In the earlier job, he had spent most of his time in acceptance testing and material review. Moving to headquarters was a big opportunity for him, and he wanted to do a particularly good job. Up to this time, he had not been given a specific assignment to tackle on his own. Working with the other staff members and going through the orientation program had been interesting, but he was getting anxious to get his teeth into a real problem.

"Tom," said his boss, "I would like you to go out to Premier Pump and take a look at their overall quality situation. Here are the primary items.

"Premier has been a member of the corporation for 1 year. It was a family-owned company, and as a matter of fact, Jon Selden is still general manager and his brother, Ed, is chief engineer. They're good men, and we're delighted that they decided to stay with us.

"Premier is a successful company and is considered the quality leader in its field, even though its prices are a little above the rest of the market. This folder will give you some information on their oganization and products. You'll have to get whatever else you need from them.

"Your assignment is to determine what steps are required to lower their costs from a quality standpoint, what can be done to eliminate rising customer complaints about product quality, and what is the best way to get Premier started on a permanent quality improvement program. The most important aspect is the cost of quality. As you know, the cost of quality is the expense of waste: how much it costs the company for rework, scrap, inspection, test warranty, field service, and so on. For many companies, it runs as high as 15 percent of sales, but we know from our experience that it doesn't need to be any more than 4 percent of sales. The amount saved becomes profit.

"Take all the time you need, but keep me informed of your problems and progress with a short note daily. I won't communicate with you unless you specifically request it. You shouldn't need more than 2 weeks, but make sure that any plans you feel need to be implemented get implemented and stay implemented.

"Our corporate policy is to permit the divisions to run their own affairs as long as they are making money. That means that whatever you get

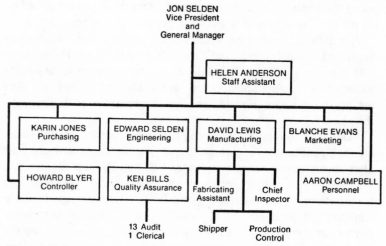

Figure 10-1

them to do will have to be done because it is right, not because it is directed."

Tom took the folder and returned to his office. Looking it over, he learned that Premier had sales of $30 million a year, returned 4.8 percent after taxes, had 1800 employees, and produced a varied line of fractional horsepower pumps that moved water, oil, milk, and about anything else that was liquid.

Their primary customers were original equipment manufacturers, but they sold about 20 percent of their product to distributors as replacements.

Their share of the market had been running a consistent 38 percent over the years. They had dropped to 32 percent in the past year, but the number of sales had held up due to the increased market. They were still the largest in their field.

An organization chart was attached (Fig. 10-1).

Tom called Jon Selden for an appointment and was assured of an enthusiastic welcome.

"We're always interested in improving our quality and will be glad to get some expert help. Of course, we can't afford to spend too much on it like they do in the space business, but I think you'll be pleased with what we are doing. Ken Bills, our quality assurance manager, will meet you at the airport to make sure you can find the plant and get settled at the motel. I'll plan on seeing you when you get in the plant tomorrow."

Ken Bills did meet Tom at the airport, and Tom was immediately impressed by Ken's energy and obvious interest in his job. He had been with Premier for 12 years, 6 years as quality assurance manager. He belonged to the American Society for Quality Control and was very active in those circles. He told Tom about his operation as they drove to the plant.

"Under our setup, manufacturing does the inspection and we evaluate their results. I have fourteen people. We run inspections and tests after manufacturing, using samples, and continually audit the product. When we find something wrong, we investigate it and then go back to manufacturing or engineering to get it fixed. Assurance reports to the engineering department so that it can be free of obligation to schedule or cost considerations. Of course, we try to be reasonable and keep the line moving. If we can't sell pumps, we don't have a job."

Tom asked about rejection rates.

"We have some good records on that," said Ken. "We're running 2.5 percent defective in receiving, 6.1 percent in fabrication shops, and 4.2 percent in final test. I know those figures because I had to brief the boss this morning. Usually we just supply monthly reports to each department head, and they discuss them at the staff meetings."

"Are those the results of manufacturing inspection and test or your results?" asked Tom.

"Those are our results. When defects are found in the production operation, the supervisor has them fixed. We feel that it is uneconomical to try to keep track of those. However, the supervisor records the rework charges and I assess all the scrap costs. We have a good feel. When we get to my office, I'll show you those figures."

The plant was a modern facility, only 2 years old. Premier had moved into it a year before selling out to XYZ. The parking lots were large, and Ken pulled into a spot with his name on it. They walked into the lobby, and Tom was given a badge to wear that said "Visitor, Tom Johnson, XYZ Headquarters."

"You can go anywhere you want with this badge. John wanted to make sure that you had all the freedom you wanted."

"Might as well wear a neon sign," thought Tom.

After introducing Tom to Jon Selden, the general manager, Ken excused himself, promising to be available whenever Tom wanted to start his plant tour.

Selden, a brisk, pleasant man, immediately put Tom at ease. After some small talk they got around to the subject at hand.

"I know your primary concern is our quality costs, and we would appreciate any help we can get along that line. However, most quality control guys only want to put in more checks and safeguards—that runs the costs up more. We're in a commercial business. Now, I always back my quality control people when they get into it with production—even when I think they're being unreasonable. That's because I want to make sure that our products are good. But if we get too involved, we're liable to inspect ourselves right out of business. Incidentally, I hope you can limit this particular evaluation to 4 or 5 days. This is the busiest part of our year."

Tom asked Selden if there was anything in particular that he could do for him while in the plant.

Jon got up and closed the door.

"There is one thing. I don't really know much about the quality business, and I'd appreciate your evaluation of Ken Bills's job performance. He's a good engineer, and I can always put him back into design if he's not the right man for the job."

"What specific things would you like me to look for?"

"My greatest concern is that the other managers don't seem to have a great deal of respect for his decisions. We must get into four or five hassles a month on whether or not something is good enough. I'd like to know why he can't handle these things."

Tom assured Jon that he would look into it and would plan to meet with him in 5 days to provide his initial impressions of the total operation, as well as to offer some recommendations for improvement. He showed the general manager the basic review format for evaluating a company's overall quality operation and told him that he would provide a complete report in that format for future reference.

His primary report, however, would be a list of specific recommendations for improvement (if there were any) and the backup information showing why these items had been selected and pointing out implementation steps as well as potential savings. Jon would have the opportunity to review the report in detail with Tom before it was submitted to head-quarters. Any comments that the general manager had would be included. Tom also pointed out that he must send a daily status report to his boss at headquarters, and asked if Jon would like to read it before it went over.

"Only if you're talking numbers. We like to make sure that all dollar figures are checked with the controller and people figures with personnel before they go to XYZ. Sometimes they get excited up there."

They shook hands after Jon had firmly told Tom that he was welcome to come see him at any time during his visit. Bills was summoned, and he led Tom back to his office. Since it was late, they agreed to start the next morning, and Tom was driven back to his motel.

The next morning, Tom rented a car and drove to the plant. He met Ken Bills in his office.

"Where would you like to start?" asked Ken.

Tom thought a bit.

"I've worked out a kind of plan, Ken. It seems to me that I should get a general understanding of your operation before we begin to get specific. Perhaps we could go over the company in terms of number and types of people and how the quality control department works, and then go on a tour of the plant so I can become familiar with your product. Then we can look at the charts you have and examine some specific problems. Let me ask you a question on that: What do you feel is your biggest problem?"

"I think my biggest problem is trying to get the manufacturing people to understand the need for high quality in our product. In fact, that's a problem with all areas. We use a lot of castings, for instance, and they're always off dimension. Purchasing says that's as good as they can get for the price we can pay. Manufacturing goes along with them and plans the machining operations to accommodate the defects. The final product works okay but it takes a lot of special checking. Then, too, when we audit the product lines and find something out of specification, they won't change anything. They just figure out a way to use it. Of course, that's not all bad; it does keep the product moving."

"What does top management say about these items?" Ken wondered.

"They don't particularly like it, but they have to go along. After all, we're in a commercial business. My boss feels we write too much down now anyway. That's why he won't issue a casting specification. We do much better giving the foundries the drawing for the final item and then working with them until they come up with a satisfactory unit."

When Tom asked about the number of people, Ken took him over to the personnel department where Tom met Aaron Campbell. They discussed the personnel distribution, and Aaron presented Tom with a chart showing departmental distribution (see below). He suggested that Tom talk with the individual department managers concerning personnel usage.

Tom asked Aaron what his biggest problem was.

"Guess it would have to be the union. We've only had a union for 2 years. It started just about the time we moved to this plant. Before that we never had any trouble. But you know the kind of workers you get today. They're only interested in money and don't really care about their work. We get twenty, maybe, twenty-five grievances a week. Usually they wind up being nothing but a lot of hot air. It's hard to make these people understand who owns the plant. But that's not the kind of stuff that interests you quality types. If I can do anything for you during your stay, please let me know."

Tom and Ken proceeded through the plant. It was generally very well laid out, and Tom, for his purposes, mentally divided it into three areas: receiving and stockroom, metal-working fabrication, and final assembly. All areas were well lighted, and people seemed to be working steadily.

Personnel Distribution

Manufacturing	
Direct labor*	1187
Indirect labor	214
Engineering	197
Purchasing	32
Personnel and labor relations	27
Marketing	67
Quality assurance	15
Labs (mechanical research)	11
General management and clerical overhead	32
TOTAL	1782

*Includes 173 inspection and test personnel.

They had an adequate amount of room. Housekeeping—except for the fabrication shop—was also adequate. As Ken said, "You can't expect a machine shop to look like someone's living room."

The Receiving Area

All incoming material arrived by truck and was placed in a receiving bay. Production control people sorted the lots as they arrived and assigned a priority to them. This was done with red, amber, and green stickers. Red had the highest priority. After the lots had been logged, they were moved to the inspection area. Expeditors with shortage lists moved the lots to the inspectors in order to ensure that the highest-priority items were handled first.

Inspection equipment was not complex—mostly mechanical gauges—and seemed to be in good order. The inspectors seemed to know their jobs. Ken said that most of them had been there for a good while and knew the parts so well that it wasn't necessary to maintain a lot of records. If they needed a print, it could be obtained from engineering in a few moments.

An average of sixty lots was received each day. The six inspectors and one tester could process about fifty a day. The difference was made up by working regular overtime.

The stockrooms were enclosed in wire cages, and all material was distributed by the production control personnel. Raw material was particularly well protected. It had to be issued in the presence of one of the receiving inspectors to make sure that the wrong material was not given out.

Ken handed Tom a chart showing the receiving rejection rate for the past year. "As you asked me before, this represents the findings by my auditor over there. She checks some of the lots going into stores on a sample basis."

"What does she do when she finds one wrong?" asked Tom.

"Let's talk to her about that."

The audit inspector explained that she selected parts at random as they came through and checked them against the purchase order and drawings to determine how well the inspectors had done. "When I find one wrong, I send it back to the inspector, to be checked again. Then it goes to stock. Mostly I check the amber and green sticker boxes. The red are hand-carried to the line, and line inspectors there can cover it."

"Do you keep a list of the rejections against each inspector? And if so, what do you do with it?"

The auditor stated that she did keep such a list and supplied it to the receiving supervisor daily. She didn't know what the receiving supervisor did with it, but assumed that it was used to rate the inspectors.

As they walked away, Tom asked Ken what happened to material rejected in the receiving inspection area and how much of that there was.

"Couldn't be very much. We only send two or three lots a month back to the suppliers. When something doesn't check out, the inspector gets together with the expeditor, and they bring a manufacturing supervisor over to see if it can be used. Sometimes they get a buyer or engineer in on it too. These are very aggressive, dedicated people, and they are quite inventive. We don't have much difficulty here. Wait until we get into assembly. That's the problem area."

Before going into the manufacturing areas, Ken introduced Tom to the manufacturing manager, Dave Lewis. Although Lewis appeared to be a real "bull-of-the-woods" type, Tom found him to be extremely practical and quite concerned about the product quality.

"My scrap and rework figures are quite low for this type of industry, I think. Yet we are still spending too much money. Last month I spent $2480 on rework alone. That is the equivalent of five people—a lot of money. My scrap was $7000."

"Do you always use the same people for rework?" asked Tom.

"In some cases we do, particularly in final assembly; it takes a real fine hand to put some of these parts together if they're a little out of dimension. The rework I was speaking of was that done by the nonrework personnel. We don't count our repair stations as rework; they're a fact of life in every company."

"You have to be practical on these things," said Ken firmly. "If we included the planned rework in our figures each period, they would look real high. How many people are involved here, Dave?"

"In fabrication, we have twelve rework people, and in final assembly around twenty-two. Of course, testers are expected to do some adjustment if they have a problem, but that doesn't include disassembly. We're laying out a new pump line, and I'm putting rework stations in three places to speed up the flow. Right now, with our present setup, we have to move the parts on and off the line."

Dave volunteered to be available whenever Tom wanted to see him.

The Fabrication Shop

Ken gave Tom the rejection data for the fabrication shop.

"We kept the data generated by manufacturing inspection for a long time, and we found that it generally ran about twice that picked up by audit. Eventually, we got enough confidence in that ratio to just use the audit numbers. I think we're on an improving trend."

The shop consisted of lathes, screw machines, and the usual satellite equipment. Inspection areas were set up in each section, and completed lots were moved to these areas. In addition, the machine operators checked the pieces as they went along. The auditors would select some lots after inspection had been completed and reexamine them. The inspector carried or carted the lots to the inspection area for this audit.

Repeating the same method as in the receiving area, Tom asked the inspector to explain the procedure. Here, the offending inspector was called to the audit area and shown the defects overlooked. Methods of inspection were compared and an agreement reached about why the error had occurred. The lot was then sent to the rework area, unless it was on the critical shortage list. Then the expeditor was called and a meeting was arranged to accept the material.

The purchasing manager, Karin Jones, found that she and Tom had several mutual friends. Karin was new with Premier, having joined them less than a year ago.

"This business is sure different than aerospace," said Karin. "Here you buy on price and delivery exclusively. You've a lot more room in the tolerances, and you don't have to live with those high-quality products. Of course, we insist that the suppliers meet the requirements; if we didn't, they'd send us junk. But where we used to have a specification an inch thick for every little detail, now we just get outline drawings, and our buyers can use a little more judgment. However, since I'm the one that gets the devil if the parts aren't right, we're very careful on this quality thing. Ken here has a screaming fit with me at least twice a week, and I think that we're beginning to go more his way.

"I get reports from his people in receiving inspection, and we try to take action on them. However, in most cases the error is missed in inspection—not much we can do about that."

"How do you pick your suppliers?" asked Tom.

"That's another advantage of the commercial business. We just write up the orders and the salespeople come in here every day. We can give the same package to two or three outfits and wait for their bids. Of course, if we have a bad experience, we don't have to go with them again. Ken has sat in on a couple of those bid conferences."

"I don't envy you those conferences," said Ken. "I'll stick to the quality business."

Final Assembly

The purchased and fabricated parts came together in the assembly area. Production control people delivered the various parts to the end of each line, where they were transferred to bins. Assembly personnel did their work, then laid the unit on a conveyer belt to carry it to the next operation. After the fabrication shop, it seemed well ordered and quiet. Tom noticed that everyone wore white coats except the supervisors and inspectors. The supervisors wore blue coats, and the inspectors red. Audit people wore blue.

"The units are given a visual inspection at the end of the line. Then they are placed on the cross-room belt and delivered to the test room. It's through this door."

Ken led Tom into a large, dust-free area, through an air lock.

The people working in this room were covered from head to foot in white and wore lint-free gloves. Twelve benches were set up on one side, and eight on the other.

"These twelve benches are for production testing operations," said Ken. "My main audit effort is on the other side. My eight people do a 100 percent test of all units before they leave. It is the same test that production does, but without the adjustments. That's why we can do it faster."

Since time was getting short, Tom suggested that they go directly to the engineering office and that perhaps they could discuss corrective action at the same time.

Ken introduced Tom to Ed Selden, the engineering manager and Ken's boss. Ed was very agreeable and freely discussed his operation with Tom. In answer to Tom's question about drawing control, Ed replied that this was vested in the individual project engineers.

"They are the ones who have to live and die with the product," said Ed, "so we give them the tools to do the job. That's one thing you'll find here. When we ask a person to do the job, we give him the tools. That's why we give the inspectors to the supervisors. It works out much better that way."

Ken discussed the corrective action system.

"Corrective action is centered around the product engineer. Each supervisor or inspector has ready access to the product engineer. If the problem falls in another area, say, purchasing or quality, the product engineer refers it to the proper department. In addition, my staff selects the problems they see, and this is placed on a monthly report to all managers by Ed. Anyone who doesn't take action after the first report gets clobbered on the second: It's been very effective."

As they talked, Tom received a call from the general manager. Jon Selden had to leave for Los Angeles at noon the next day and would be gone for a week. He wondered if Tom was well enough along to discuss his findings the next morning, and if so, would Tom mind if the staff was invited to participate. Tom agreed.

Two days later Tom was back in headquarters sheepishly admitting that his trip had been a failure.

In Retrospect

It must be apparent to anyone who has had anything to do with a manufacturing operation that Premier management runs a sloppy shop and that their controls are nonexistent. In his meeting with the staff, Tom Johnson pointed out that rejection rates were incomplete and biased; inspection, testing, and rework were all excessive; some drawing control must be exercised; the quality manager could do with higher personal standards; and many, many other things. So many improvements were needed that Tom got carried away.

Selden and his team were very upset with his suggestions and closed their ears to such criticism coming from someone with such limited exposure to Premier. The meeting, held to explain his findings, became quite cool in a hurry, and Tom returned to headquarters frustrated with his failure.

He deserved what happened to him. He worked diligently at detecting and listing the details that must be corrected. However, he did this on the unwarranted assumption that the Premier management wanted to correct such deficiencies. Nothing could have been further from the truth. They had no desire to improve. They hadn't asked him to come. They thought everything was just great. Once the market recovered, they'd be right back up there on top again.

You know that's not going to happen, Tom knows it, and so does everyone but the managers who count. Therefore, they must be made to see that they can obtain instant rewards now, in their own operation, without waiting for the fickle marketplace or the good fairy.

What measurable items interest them? In this case, profit is the only thing. Their profit is not very high and is slipping fast. Tom should have asked himself what he could do to increase that profit before attempting to "sell" his program.

He should have calculated the cost of doing things wrong, the method his boss suggested. If you add up the expenses involved in inspection, testing, quality control, rework, scrap, and warranty (and they probably are not including half of it), you will arrive at a figure that represents close to 10 percent of the sales dollar. The actual figures probably would bring it to 15 percent.

Tom knew that these costs should run less than 4 percent of sales. The difference between these figures is attractive enough to get anyone's attention. There is little or no difficulty in attaining these cost levels, and probably improving the product conformance in the bargain.

If, by chance, these should be super-hardheads, Tom still has the option of returning home to state that he offered them a chance to pick up $1.5 to $3 million, and let his boss go into the Situation Management business.

Too many staff people fail in their activities because they try to sell the incidental instead of the prime item. Anything can be measured if you are willing to think about it for a while.

Here is what Tom should have done prior to the meeting:

SITUATION ANALYSIS GUIDE

Awareness

1. What seems to be the situation?   Premier Pump

Management runs a very ineffective operation; yet

they are not interested in improvement. If I

can't get them to improve, I am in trouble.

2. How did I find out that the situation exists?
After spending some time at their plant and meet-

ing their management people, it became apparent to

me that this was the case.

3. What is the potential effect of this matter?
This is my first big assignment; if I fail, there

may be no more. I will be back in a plant some-

where, doing time studies.

4. How serious is it?   Critical.

---

5.   How much time do I have to extricate myself?
The meeting will be tomorrow morning; I only have

a few hours.

Evaluation

1.   What evidence leads me to believe that the situation exists?   The management is shipment-oriented. They

don't really care about quality; inspection only

checks items that are not needed at the moment.

Housekeeping is terrible; the personnel manager

thinks people are no damn good; the quality con-

trol manager is weak. Their quality costs are not

calculated, but if you add up the people and costs

involved, just roughly, it is at least 11 percent

of sales.

2.   What is the specific source of this evidence?
My own observations while being carefully guided

around the plant. Heaven knows what is really go-

ing on that I didn't see.

3.   Do I know whether the evidence is factual?
Yes, I have seen and witnessed it myself.

4.   Can I list the steps that created the situation?

This was a family-owned company with a unique product and no competition. The customers had to take what they got. Over the years competition set in, and their share of the market began to diminish. However, they did nothing to reduce their costs or improve their product. The world is passing them by.

5.   Whose mind must I change to resolve the problem?

John Selden's first of all, but the entire management team thinks the same way.

6.   What does that mind think now?

They think that if they go on the way they have, the market will change and they will get back their share, perhaps with a price increase. They also think their operation method is just grand.

7.   How will I know when the situation is resolved?

When they accept a list of the improvements I think are necessary and set about doing them enthusiastically, even to the point of adding some of their own.

Action

1. Relate the key individuals to the key issues.
The management doesn't think they need to improve.

2. Why do they believe this?   They have seen no
evidence that it is in their best interest to
change their style of operating.

**3. What would it require to separate them from this
belief?**   Some specific evidence that if they
change their ways, their results will be dramatically better.

4. What is the best method to use in this separation?
The only thing I have going for me is the calcula-
tion that they are spending 11 percent of sales
for the cost of quality instead of the 4 percent
we know is possible. The difference is 1.8
million bucks.

5. How do I implement the method?   I forget all
of the other things I have to tell them about
their operation and give the cost to them
straight. If they are not interested, then I'll
let my boss do it.

6.   Once it is over, what steps do I take to ensure that it will never happen again?   I'll help them install a better cost report system so that they won't get so far off the track again.

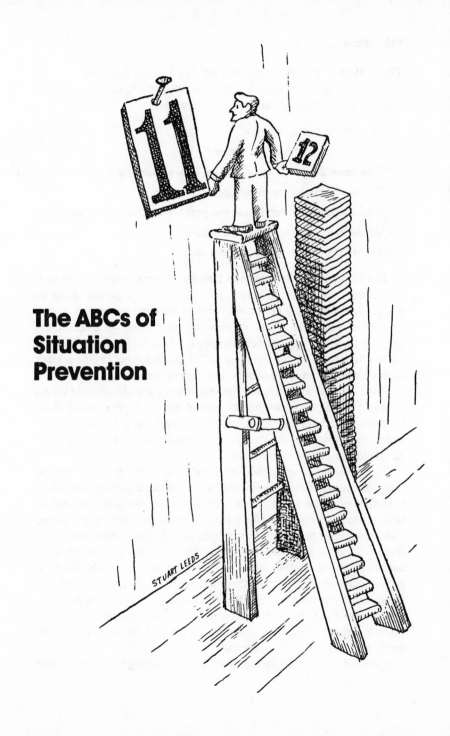

The ABCs of Situation Prevention

STUART LEEDS

The folklore of all nations has at least one thing in common: it is well stocked with adages designed to pass on wisdom accrued by the experience of living. Most of these refer to prevention:

"A stitch in time saves nine."

"Marry in haste, repent at leisure."

"The more things change, the more they remain the same."

"Those who marry for money earn every cent."

"Those who cannot remember the past are condemned to repeat it."

"As the twig is bent, so grows the tree."

"A wise man builds his house on a rock."

The list goes on; everyone has a favorite. You may note that although the sayings are repeated often, and solemnly, the person doing so doesn't feel they apply personally. They're for other people.

That is what makes situation prevention so difficult—the rules don't apply to us. When we consider marrying in haste, we justify our decision by another adage: "Love conquers all." If we decide not to take a stitch at this particular time, we quote: "Don't tarry, tomorrow is here."

It will do little good to follow the rest of this particular thought unless we can convince ourselves that the procedures for staying out of trouble by systematically preventing it apply to us personally. We are inclined to feel that others impose situations upon us instead of seeing ourselves as creators of our own difficulties.

The modern-day equivalent of avoiding a "stitch in time" can be found in every business, be it a real estate office, a grocery store, or a manufacturing plant. The inevitability of this avoidance can be noticed when a manager sighs from the fatigue of strain and worry and mutters, "We never have time to do things right, but we always have time to fix them." Certainly an astute observation. Obviously the observation is not believed because no effort is made to change it. Managers think the next program will be different, that there will be more notice or more time or fewer unknowns involved. So they don't examine past errors to determine where things began to go wrong. Somehow management doesn't seem to include taking time to learn from the mistakes so that the next batch of problems can be prevented.

We must make some attempt to change this feeling instead of looking at prevention as an emotional item of judgment. Let's try to put it in a cold, impersonal way: *Prevention is planned anticipation.* (This should not be confused with being a worry wart.) We can anticipate without becoming emotionally involved.

Probably the most dramatic application of planned anticipation is the system management technique used in the space and weapons industries (a technique used only because the customer absolutely demanded it). Apollo scientists worked out every detailed step necessary to get to the moon and back long before the first piece of needed hardware was developed. Each step, measured in microseconds, was then examined for its content and for its effect on the next step (as well as the total system), and then given to a group to develop. All known or anticipated problems were identified and resolved before the system was committed to.

Very few of us have the resources available to conduct complete system-management analysis or to construct a computerized PERT chart before we move out on our normal actions. However, it is possible to train ourselves to use the computer in our heads and consider the future effects of our planned actions in order to see what might happen. We do it sometimes. Most often we don't. Have you ever:

Run out of gasoline?

Bought something that turned out to be worthless?

Missed a plane?

Had a customer return an item because it didn't function properly?

Burned a dinner?

Driven 60 miles out of your way?

Been ditched romantically?

Been involved in an accident?

Been surprised by what someone thought?

Most of us have done these things or had them happen to us. Most of us will agree that the situations could have been prevented if we had taken a moment to review our program before acting. Consumer bureaus state that very few people are swindled if they resist the opportunity to "buy now because the offer expires at midnight."

What is the logical extension of planned anticipation? It is anticipating potential disaster on a routine basis, preferably by following a procedure of quick evaluation.

Situation Prevention logic is keyed by three questions. If each is considered for but a microsecond prior to commitment, the chance of avoiding problems is good. If each is considered for a total of 30 seconds, the probability of avoidance is excellent. Concentration for 2 minutes guarantees results.

These questions are:

---

1. What are the short- and long-range purposes of this action?

2. Have I prepared the way for the successful completion of this action by establishing communications and coordination with those who will be affected?

3. Is the implementation method I have chosen the result of a thoughtful situation analysis, including "best" and "worst" anticipated results, or am I following normal practices?

Let's take a simple, everyday case as an example. You are driving down a six-lane freeway in the fast, or inside, lane. All lanes are crowded, but the traffic is moving in an orderly fashion. You are alert and attentive since you must turn off within the next few miles.

The warning sign for your turnoff appears overhead, and you know that you must leave the highway from the far right-hand lane in 2 miles. That means a six-lane change. It is time to start moving over. You flash your directional signal and look for room in the next lane in order to work your way across.

---

1. Question: What are the short- and long-range purposes of this action?

   Answer: The short-range purpose is to place yourself in a position to cross the six lanes so that you can exit 2 miles down the road. The long-range purpose is to get to your final destination safely.

2. Question: Have I prepared the way for the successful completion of these actions by establishing communications and coordination with those who will be affected?

Answer: I have opened communication with the other drivers affected by flashing my directional signal in order to indicate my desire to change lanes. However, I must recognize that this is strictly a one-way communication, since I have no way of evaluating their willingness to permit me to do this. Therefore, as I cross I have to carefully evaluate the intentions of each driver around me.

3. Question: Is the implementation method I have chosen the result of a thoughtful situation analysis, including "best" and "worst" anticipated results, or am I following normal practices?

   Answer: This exit was chosen by me before I ever got on the highway. It was recommended by a friend, but I am stuck with it. The best thing that can happen is that I will successfully cross the six lanes in the minute and a half allocated. The worst thing that can happen is that I may cause an accident that will exterminate me and several others right there on the spot.

In between these two extremes lie two options—go on to the next exit (and work out a situation analysis guide to explain being late), or forget the whole thing (the coward's way).

The important analysis in this case is the comparison between the reward for success and the penalty for failure. They are too far apart. It may be better to consider moving to the next exit and circling back, with its resultant loss in time, than to be a stubborn planner and force your way to the exit in too short a time. Your next trip will be easier because you will know that you must be in the right lane earlier than you anticipated.

The value of these questions lies in forcing ourselves to review our thinking and opportunities in a routine fashion in order to avoid an illogical act. The time required is relatively short, once the meaning and usefulness of the considerations are clear. Let's examine them in greater depth by using the Situation Prevention Guide.

---

1. What are the short- and long-range purposes of this action?

   We all seem to have our own definitions of PURPOSE. (I have placed it in capital letters because that is the way it seems to be viewed, as some noble abstract or spiritual sort of thing.) Disraeli said: "The secret of success is constancy to purpose." Shakespeare reported: "The flighty purpose never is o'ertook unless the deed go with it." Carlyle laid it out in lifetime terms: "The man without a purpose is like a ship without a rudder—a waif, a nothing, a no man. Have a purpose in life and, having it, throw such strength of mind and muscle into your work as God has given you."

We all have some purpose in life, something we want to accomplish, something we believe in—whether we can clearly state it or not—but that does not enter into this discussion. Lifetime purposes should be used for the guidance of conscience and habit. The kind of purpose we are considering now refers to the specific task at hand and its objectives. We are concerned with: Why do you want to do this? What do you want to get out of it?

Much of the wasted effort in human activity is a result of a lack of clear definition of the real or total reason for doing something. If you cannot determine why you are doing something, you probably won't do it very well.

In stating the real purpose, you must be specifically honest with yourself—no one else needs to know. If you ask a business manager why the plan is to expand a certain function, you will hear about reducing exposure, increasing profitability, and moving into new markets. The real purpose may be to make vice president.

Don't miss the opportunity to expose your real purpose to yourself.

2. Have I prepared the way for the successful completion of this action by establishing positive communications and coordination with those who will be affected?

("But, Orville, I thought you were going to put the gasoline in.")

In game or war situations, it is considered proper to keep the competition from knowing the purpose of your program. As a result, it is sometimes not possible to tell your own people.

In matters of high corporate strategy, a similar situation may present itself. Some corporations are more secretive than the Armed Forces in this day of mergers and competition. Unfortunately, they sometimes exaggerate the depth of the "competition" and don't tell anyone.

In the normal business and personal situations we face, it is vital to share our scheme with those who will be affected by it (and therefore will find out anyway). The amount of active interest a person takes in another's plans is proportional to how early in their execution or development that person becomes part of the process (Law 4). Active interest usually means help, or at least lack of interference; so it is a vital thing to stimulate.

To communicate properly you must, of course, know what you are doing or plan to do. Then you must be able to state this purpose in a way that those involved will be able to understand. After this, you must develop a measurement method that is acceptable and that can be used to let people determine progress.

All these things are of little use unless you can determine with whom you want to communicate, what you want them to know, and what you want them to do about it.

This one item has to be the biggest problem in the communications activity. You have to be very careful to determine who can positively or adversely affect your operation, even though it might be by doing nothing. History is full of stories where a little nameless, faceless person, who wasn't informed or considered, caused the fall of the mighty. The mishap of the nail that held the horseshoe, or didn't hold the horseshoe, probably occurred because no one told the blacksmith that this was an important horse; and the blacksmith was relying on warranty and the laws of probability to guarantee his reputation.

If you plan to do something, you must consider the effect it will have on others. Not only the others who appear on the organization chart, but all those who will be affected. And you must pass the information to them in a context that appeals to their interest.

Many a plant manager has busily announced: "Parking Lot 3 will be closed," only to find that the employees interpreted this to mean that the third shift was going to be laid off. After all, that's where they normally park. What the announcement was really trying to say was: "Parking Lot 3 will be closed for 6 weeks while it is being repaved."

Pride: that is the item you must be concerned with when determining with whom to communicate. Almost every conflict of the human race throughout the years has been caused by real or implied impugning of pride. No one can stand to be ignored. Everyone wants part of the action.

Whose pride would be affected by your project?

Let's suppose that Carol is the owner of a clothing store. Business is fairly good, but not good enough. She needs a little something to spur things on; hence, she decides that she will issue gold-plated charge cards to the "significant" people in the community. This, she thinks, will make them very conscious of the store's presence and the respect with which their patronage is held. A list of prestigious people is prepared, and cards are sent out by the advertising agency. Then she sits back and anticipates the profits.

The next thing you know, business is off. Not only is business off, but the clerks are snarly, the credit manager is having a snit, and some of her oldest customers are giving Carol the cold shoulder. How could this happen from such good intentions? Why should these people be acting so strangely? Poor Carol!

The clerks are upset because Carol didn't give them the chance to put some of their valued (but lower-class) personal customers on the list for this status symbol; the credit manager is unhappy because he didn't get to run the credit checks and issue the cards (he knows Carol will hold him responsible for any delinquent accounts that might result); and the old customers are upset because Carol obviously took them for granted since she did not include them in the new program.

Test: Select one reaction that isn't a function of pride.

The age of unilateral action is past. There are no "all-powerful" managers any more. There is very little that even the most determined person can accomplish alone. Even the assassin must have a victim. Our lives are wrapped up in an ever-changing "who's who" of those we deal with.

In selecting the "who," you must consciously determine a list of those whose pride could be affected by any action. You can think in groups if you are so inclined, but you must be careful not to omit anyone. For instance:

Harvey Stockton was elected to his state legislature at the age of 24, the youngest man ever to accomplish that feat. He was personable, articulate, energetic, intelligent, well educated, and he obviously had a great future before him. Some people were already concerned that the state constitution required the governor to be at least 30 years old. Harvey was approached by several lobbyists with discreet offers of large returns for minimal effort. He sent them scurrying, and, in one case, personally arrested the offender and turned him in to the state attorney general.

One day, a group of chicken farmers approached Harvey concerning the lack of a sufficient bounty on chicken hawks. Because no one actively pursued these birds in order to collect the meager bounty, they were multiplying rapidly and destroying chickens at a record rate throughout the state. The farmers showed Harvey figures to prove their point.

He was irate and immediately dropped a bill into the hopper to raise the bounty. He made a stirring speech in the legislature in favor of the bill. The increased bounty was soundly defeated, and along with it his chance of future political achievement. It seems that the hawks weren't really that active. As a matter of fact, the bird conservation club (whose membership consisted of every major industrialist and politician in the state) was desperately trying to find a way to save the species. They did not look too happily on the judgment of the new legislator. Soon, even the lobbyists were not speaking to him.

3. Is the implementation method I have chosen the result of a thoughtful situation analysis, including "best" and "worst" anticipated results, or am I following normal practices?

The more creative you are in conceiving new situations, the more you must attend to the danger of using the accepted or normal approach. New ideas require new implementation methods. They require an estimate of total reaction. Rousseau entered into a literary discussion of the rights of man. His purpose was to question the thinking of the French Academy. His result was to incite the French Revolution. Luther wanted more say about church policy being planned on a local level. His result was a bifurcation of the existing church.

Whether these happenings were good or bad in their total effect has nothing to do with our discussion. What really matters is that neither Situation Manager got what he had planned and, in effect, created a happening beyond his power to control.

The pragmatist regards each new device from the standpoint of "What does it do?" By this method, everything is reduced to its mechanical base. We can then judge its worth on the effect it will have on costs, output, safety, and so on. This works well with devices.

Since we are concerned with people situations, we must ask ourselves two similar questions concerning our planned method or technique of implementing the scheme:

What is the worst thing that can happen?

What is the best thing that can happen?

Unless these evaluations are consciously conducted, you will not be prepared to react to early measurements of your program's success or failure. Not only that, you won't have the absolute evaluation of whether or not you want to take the step at all.

In preparing your speech before the AFL-CIO national convention, you might decide to make a strong plea for the legal abolishment of all labor unions. Upon reflection, you conclude that the best thing that could happen would be for your audience to politely ignore what to them would be an outrageous suggestion. The worst (and probable) happening would be that you would be torn limb from limb right there in the auditorium. Since the result is obvious in advance, you might temper your remarks (if you're bound to make them) to a recommendation that the union leaders consider an approach other than the one they are now using—said approach to be based on the accumulated wisdom present before you. The difference is that instead of being considered a hopeless radical, you now become a statesman, and the union leaders just might do something.

The situations in Chapters 12 and 13 are intended to permit a closer examination of the situation-prevention concepts discussed above.

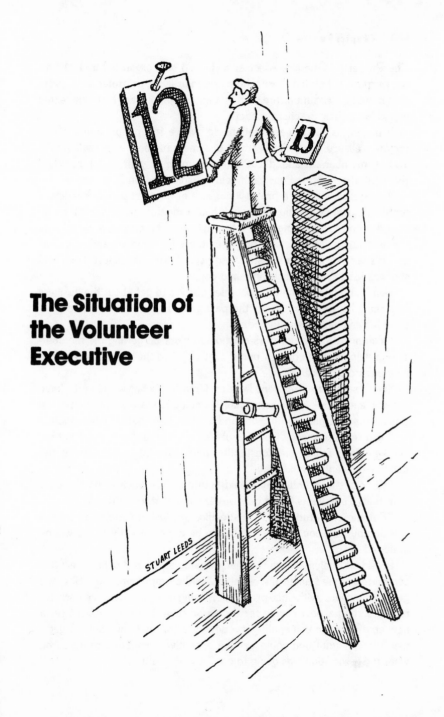

The Situation of the Volunteer Executive

STUART LEEDS

The Property Managers Association (PMA) was organized in 1949 for the purpose of helping those who made their living as professional property managers communicate with one another and share techniques that would keep their practices modern.

It began, as all such associations do, with a few people and an inadequate treasury. Over the years, it became a national organization with 13,500 members. It added 1000 new members a year, which matched the 1000 that dropped out each year for some reason or other.

The association had a professional staff of fourteen people headquartered in Columbus, Ohio, and published a monthly magazine that contained reports of meetings and a few articles. The executive director of the association, Tom Nelson, had been there for 25 years and was retiring. His secretary, Vera Walston, had been there since before Tom, and she was leaving also. Their time had come.

Tom had been urging the volunteer officers to get about the business of picking his replacement for the past year. He had no desire to postpone leaving while they fiddled.

"You need a younger person who can work on getting the membership growing and the budget under control," said the past president and now director, Hansen Bills.

"No," said Vice President Lawson Ontario, "what we have to have is a whole new look at the association. I think that we should put a professional property manager in there and get this association moving again."

"You're both wrong," said Carol Vernon, also a director. "What we need to do is follow the constitution and bring this matter up at the national convention next May."

"We can't wait until May," said Hansen. "We have to do it sooner than that. Tom wants to get out to Arizona and start retiring."

"But the constitution is very specific," persisted Carol. "You can't just do anything you want. It all has to be done correctly or we will be criticized."

President Evelyn Johnson sat back wearily as the rest of her executive committee argued about the situation for the umpteenth time. She was getting nowhere with this problem. Picking a new executive director meant setting a new course for the association, but you couldn't set a new course unless you could get a new director, and you couldn't get a new director until you could get the executive committee to agree on what the association was going to be like in the future.

The "old guard" was jealous of its prerogatives and did not want the PMA to change in the slightest. They kept control by intimidating the newer officers and by quoting the constitution and bylaws to prove their points. When Evelyn appointed a constitutional committee, it found that many of these quotes were not factual. But the effect was still the same. All this quarreling took time and moved the problem along not at all. Each positive suggestion was met with a negative response. Each attempt to bring something to a vote was met with sulking and petulance. They were going nowhere.

"We really should get together with the board on this," muttered Carol. "This is a matter that should be presented to the whole board for discussion. It is just too important for us to do ourselves."

"If we get the board involved," replied Lawson, "they will just argue and fight for the whole meeting and get nothing done."

"Well, we sure aren't getting anywhere like this. Some of us are afraid to move, some of us don't know what to move to, and a few just want to get it all over with," growled Hansen.

Evelyn shut it all out in her mind. "I sure would like to get it all over with," she thought. "If only there were some way to stop this eternal wrangling. Even when it comes time to vote on something, they split half and half and want me to decide. We will be at this forever."

Evelyn tapped her pencil on the glass and, when quiet had resulted, said: "I would like to get back to the agenda. We have to make some policy on three specific items and then prepare to take action. I have checked the constitution carefully; we do not need to take this to the board or to the members. We can decide, the five of us, officially. And of course Tom has an unofficial vote.

"Here are the three items we need to resolve. First, shall we advertise for a professional association manager, or shall we select someone from inside the profession of property management to be our executive director? Second, shall we limit association membership to those who have practiced the profession for 5 years, as the constitution states now, or shall we reduce the requirement to 1 year? Third, shall we appoint a constitutional revision committee to update our controlling document, or shall we go on as is?

"These are the three agenda items we have assigned ourselves, and these are the three items we are going to get answered one way or another.

"Since all of the executive committee members are at this moment raising their hands to be recognized, I will call for a 10-minute recess while we think this over."

Evelyn walked down the hall to the rest room and composed her thoughts. It was obvious that all of this was going to take forever. They were never going to settle these items because they all were so determined to satisfy their own small interests. They really didn't care about the association at all, just themselves. They were afraid that somehow the control of the PMA, or their part of it, might slip from their grasp. She was determined that this would be absolutely her last term in service to any organization in any form.

In desperation, she returned to the meeting room, opened her briefcase, and took out the Situation Analysis Guide. "As a last resort," she mumbled. Then, ignoring the argument in the corner of the room, she began painfully and honestly to fill out the form.

SITUATION ANALYSIS GUIDE

Awareness

1. What seems to be the situation?   The members of the executive committee are in complete disagreement on the agenda items.

2. How did I find out that the situation exists?
All you have to do is be here; they argue all day and don't listen to each other.

3. What is the potential effect of this matter?
Very serious. It means that the PMA is ungovern-

able.   Individual concerns are all that matter; no

one is thinking of the members.

4. How serious is it?   It could mean that we will

just flounder forever.

5. How much time do I have to extricate myself?
We need to get it changed today. If it goes to

the board, we will never get it settled.

Evaluation

**1. What evidence leads me to believe that the situation
exists?**   Watching and listening. If you look at

the minutes of the meetings for the past several

years, nothing changed much.

2. What is the specific source of this evidence?
Personal observation and the comments of con-

cerned members.

3. Do I know whether the evidence is factual?
Yes, no doubt about it.

4. Can I list the steps that created the situation?
No one else will do much work in the association,

so these people just kept getting reelected. Now
they think it is their association. All they see
are their personal rivalries and concerns. They
can't look objectively at the association in any
way.

5. Whose mind must I change to resolve the problem?
The minds of the people on this committee: George
Welpt, Lawson Ontario, Hansen Bills, and Carol
Vernon. Tom Nelson has to agree also, or he will
kill whatever I want to do by getting George and
Carol to be against it.

6. What does that mind think now?   They think that
they alone are protecting the association from
losing control or entering into some plot of the
Devil. They really look at the whole thing very
narrowly.

7. How will I know when the situation is resolved?
When we can consider an issue on the merits of
that issue alone rather than on how it affects
members of the committee personally.

Action

1. Relate the key individuals to the key issues.
The executive committee members are more concerned about themselves than they are about the association. Their view is too narrow.

2. Why do they believe this?
They helped build the PMA and were concerned about local issues like behavior patterns of the staff or the price of magazine paper or who would head up which committee. They are not used to being broad-based officers.

3. What would it require to separate them from this belief?
I would have to get them to place the association's interests and the benefit to the members ahead of their personal concerns.

4. What is the best method to use in this separation?
They would have to become more of the whole and less of the individual. Perhaps if I insist that all agreements require that the vote be unanimous, then they wouldn't be able to position themselves to direct blame. They would have to think of the

PMA and its future first or admit that they were

hopelessly self-centered.

---

5. How do I implement the method?   I will just

announce that we have a new rule on agenda items.

We are going to implement only items that have

been unanimously agreed upon.

---

6. Once it is over, what steps do I take to ensure that it will never happen again?   I guess there is no real

way except to keep the officers revolving so

people aren't able to make the jobs their own.

Having put all of this down, Evelyn decided to make certain that she wasn't starting up another situation, so she took out the Prevention Guide just to be sure.

SITUATION PREVENTION GUIDE

1. What are the short- and long-range purposes of this action?   The short-range purpose is to get the

three agenda items agreed to and started on their

way to completion; the long-range purpose is to

try and set a new management atmosphere for this

association so the executive committee and then

the board can become effective. This should be a

fun job instead of just a big pain.

**2. Have I prepared the way for the successful comple-
tion of this action by establishing communications and
coordination with those who will be affected?**
I am going to make a speech about this and coax

them into it. I think they will see that to be

unanimous requires a lot of listening and discus-

sion. To just vote and be for or against some-

thing forever requires nothing but emotion. Some-

how I think they will understand that.

**3. Is the implementation method I have chosen the re-
sult of a thoughtful situation analysis, including "best"
and "worst" anticipated results, or am I following normal
practices?** I hope so. The worst thing that can

happen to me is that I wind up with a committee

that can't get along with each other, and I have

that now. Perhaps I will get lucky and they will

impeach me. The best thing would be that they

would suddenly see their jobs more broadly, and

we could all concentrate on what is best for the

association.

"Do you mean," asked Hansen Bills, "that any vote that all of us don't agree on will not be recorded as affirmative? Even if it is five to one?"

"That," said Evelyn, "is exactly what I mean."

"The constitution forbids that," said Carol. "It's illegal."

"No, it isn't," stated Lawson. "There is no requirement for anything but a majority, but it doesn't limit it to that."

"Well, I have to admit that our president has stated the case very clearly, and it is obvious that we are getting nowhere the way we are running things, so I say let's give it a try," said George.

The subject of whether to decide on hunting for a professional association manager or a professional property manager to take Tom's place took 2 hours of earnest discussion. However, the discussion was almost unemotional, as it began to dawn on each member that they could not be bypassed through some administrative procedure. Their vote would have to be respected; they could not be buried by a contrived majority.

Suddenly listening took place. Suddenly each of the members were concerned to hear what the others had to say. Suddenly it was a whole new, and interesting, ball game.

The second and third agenda items required less than an hour each. At the end, the entire executive committee was sitting around smiling at itself. Evelyn felt that they were on the road to a new era of management.

The last decision they made before adjourning was to see if they could try this management style out on the board. That would be a real test.

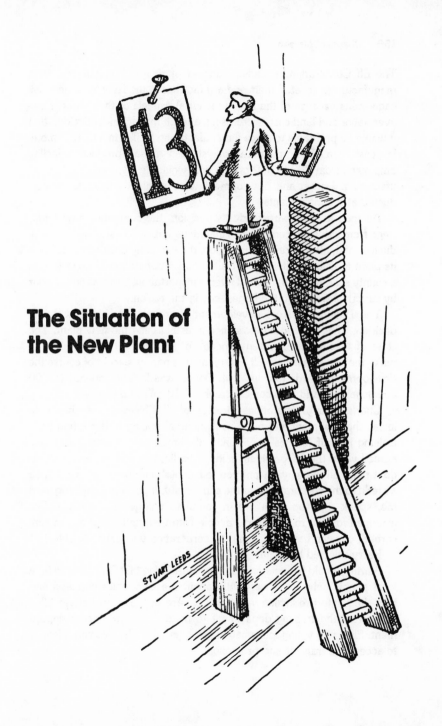

The Situation of
the New Plant

The Elf Corporation, a leading supplier of relays to electronic-system manufacturers, located their primary facilities in the New York and Chicago areas because of the highly technical aspects of their work. However, labor and land costs were rising, and Elf management decided that it would be profitable to place a manufacturing facility in a more remote, low-cost area. Their plan was to establish a mass-production facility employing from 300 to 500 people who would be involved only in manufacturing. Design and development work would continue to be conducted at the main plants.

As soon as the board made its decision, the company came under siege from industrial commissions in various states. Site studies were conducted, and, after careful deliberation, the company decided to establish its plant in Dalton, Missibama. Dalton had a population of 25,000, was a county seat, had both rail and river transportation, and was only 1 hour by superhighway from the largest city in the region.

The Dalton industrial development board was delighted with the decision. They offered all assistance in establishing the new plant. The state of Missibama allocated various tax and property concessions to make the move easier for Elf. Everyone was happy, except of course the development boards that lost out. Dalton was looking forward to 500 additional jobs and an income increase of $8 million a year.

Charles Barry, operations director of Elf-Chicago, was chosen to install the new plant and serve as its general manager. Barry had been training himself for this opportunity all through his career. He readily agreed when the Elf president said, "Charlie, this time we are going to do it right, all the way. I want you to establish an operation that will be a credit to the corporation and the community. If you need anything from me, speak right up. You are in complete charge of the move. I've arranged for you to take thirty people with you, and as far as I'm concerned, you can have anyone in the corporation you want. Good luck!"

Barry selected his team.

Staffing would be a major problem, considering that Barry had to take local people (who knew very little about the electronics business) and turn them into production workers. Because of this, Barry chose Ellen Gray from the training department to head up the personnel department. Ellen was young, personable, and energetic. She was very pleased to accept the transfer and promotion.

Frank Schlick, the manufacturing director, had worked for Barry in Chicago. No one in the business knew more than Schlick about setting up assembly operations. Schlick was happy with his new job because it represented an opportunity rarely given to men nearing retirement.

Carol Bergan, also from Chicago, joined the team as quality-control and test manager. Barry felt that her major contribution to the team would be her technical competence. Bergan was not particularly pleased about leaving Chicago, but recognized an opportunity when she saw it.

Headquarters supplied a public relations specialist, Milo Park, to assist Barry through the first year or so. He had recently joined the company after several years at an advertising agency.

Veteran managers were selected for purchasing, production control, and manufacturing engineering.

When the staff selection was complete, the move to Dalton was started. Through cooperation with Dalton real estate people, all transferred employees were settled comfortably, and the operation began.

After several days of discussion and planning, Barry and his team published their operations plan (Figure 13-1). They stuck to it carefully, updating when necessary.

For the first year, until the new plant was built, Elf used warehouse space in the city to begin production, train the people, and get established. They were never quite able to reach the output as planned, but Barry felt that this was due to the facilities and that things would be different when they moved into the new plant. The plant was being constructed by a St. Louis firm that specialized in electronic assembly layouts. It would be the most modern in the region. In fact, it would be the most modern in the relay business.

Eight months after moving into the new plant, Charles Barry was called back to headquarters as staff assistant to the manufacturing director. This job was traditionally held open for executives who had failed. It gave them time to find another job, whether they wanted one or not.

Barry could not understand why he had been pulled off the job. True, the plant output had never reached the level anticipated; true, the plant had been unionized almost immediately; and true, it was difficult to get management people to stay in Dalton. He asked the president for specific reasons for his apparent failure, but received nothing but generalities. The company was just unhappy with the progress of the operation.

Figure 13-1. Operations plan for the Elf Corporation.

	Jul.				Aug.				Sep.				Oct.				Nov.				Dec.				Jan.				Feb.				Mar.				Apr.			
	1	2	3	4	1	2	3	4	1	2	3	4	1	2	3	4	1	2	3	4	1	2	3	4	1	2	3	4	1	2	3	4	1	2	3	4	1	2	3	4
Set up office	×																																							
Move key personnel to Dalton	×																																							
Obtain temporary manufacturing space	×	×																																						
Open personnel office			×																																					
Inventory established					×	×																																		
Develop manufacturing schedules					×	×															×	×																		
Install equipment							×			×															×	×														
Train personnel							×		×																															
Start production										×																														
Ground breaking — new plant											×																													
Start construction												×			×																									
Plant layout verification											×			×																										
Board of directors visits												×		×																										
First product shipment												×		×																									×	
New equipment approval													×				×																							
Management club meetings																×	×				×								×								×			
Start policy guidebook																×	×																							
Production scheduling meetings								×	×	×			×				×				×	×			×				×	×			×	×			×	×		
Start move to new plant																														×										
Move completed																															×									
Clean up temporary building and return																																	×							
Dedication—new plant																																				×				
Train personnel																																		×					×	
First product shipment																																				×				×

The new general manager requested a task force from corporate head-quarters and started the rebuilding job. Barry was bewildered.

Perhaps we could help Mr. Barry if we discussed his program.

Q. Mr. Barry, how did you see your job?

A. My immediate purpose was to establish a new plant that would start making a profit at the earliest opportunity. To do this, it was neces-sary to staff it, train people, create an inventory, and begin to man-ufacture. My long-range purpose was to have the plant continue to function and improve over the years until it became the most prof-itable in the corporation.

Q. What priority did you use in establishing your operation?

A. My first step, of course, was picking my team. Since the plant was to be used primarily for manufacturing, I wanted a strong manufac-turing team. I had to make do with less experienced managers in the service areas. Second, I wanted to be sure that our facility would be ready on time and well designed. So we picked a St. Louis company to develop and build the plant. They brought their experienced peo-ple in and did the job in record time. Everyone admits that there isn't a better-laid-out plant in the corporation. We won a building maga-zine award for plant design, too.

The third step, and it actually was parallel to the second, was the creation of a basic manufacturing setup, the hiring and training of people, and the producing of the actual output. We had to use tem-porary buildings, but it worked out all right. We hired local people as much as we could and used the state employment commission to help us weed them out so we could get the most promising ones. These people are not used to manufacturing, you know. They have primarily a farming culture there. We were forced to bring in some technical people. We did establish a school for electronics and even made it free, but we didn't get much attendance.

The last priority was to start meeting the output requirements. I think that these were unrealistic. It isn't possible to have an uninter-rupted schedule when you are moving a line several hundred miles.

Q. How did the local people react to the plant?

A. That was a strange thing. At first they were quite enthusiastic. I went to a couple of chamber of commerce meetings and sent my industrial relations manager to speak at the Rotary. But the people never did seem to accept us. I guess it takes a few years. I had a brief conversation with the bank's management about getting some better loan terms for our transferred employees. They didn't seem to think that much could be done, and it wasn't. However, there has been good social acceptance in the community; some of our people are on the board of the country club and are quite at home.

Q. I hope you won't mind my asking. If you had it all to do over again, would you do anything differently?

A. I don't think so. I gave this thing a lot of thought before, during, and after going down there. I felt then, and I feel now, that my actions were in the interest of the corporation. It is a real mystery to me that they feel I failed. For my own peace of mind, I am going to charge the whole thing off to office politics and try again. If you'll excuse me, I must get to a meeting.

At this point, it would be interesting to evaluate the brief questioning of Mr. Barry against the three considerations of Situation Prevention to see if it might give us an insight into his failure. He doesn't feel he failed, but his employers do. Since keeping the boss satisfied with your performance is part of Situation Management, we must conclude that he did indeed fail, even if the reason is not clear.

---

1. What are the short- and long-range purposes of this action?

Barry listed his purpose as establishing a plant to make a profit, staff it, and eventually have it be the most efficient in the corporation. This is a slightly condensed quote, but I think that was the intent of his statement.

His president stated the purpose as: "Charlie, this time we are going to do it right, all the way. I want you to establish an operation that will be a credit to the corporation and the community."

Charlie didn't include anything in his purpose about doing it right and apparently didn't try to find out what that meant. He interpreted "credit to the corporation" as being profit-oriented, but did not consider "credit to the community."

Right or wrong, Charlie and his boss started out with different opinions concerning how to measure the total success of the project. Barry would have to be awful lucky to come out with the proper result, and he was too good at his job to be lucky. He spent his effort on the purpose he had chosen. Even if he had achieved it, his president might have thought him a failure. Let's ask the president what he felt the purpose was. (Apparently he could benefit from a little Situation Prevention study too.)

"I wanted to set up this plant as a showplace. It seemed to me that we could present an example of how complex electronic devices could be made in a rural area, and we would be able to eventually move our entire operations to the South. If we kept the plants small enough, we would be able to have old-fashioned employee participation and produce at a constant rate. All we would need up here in the high-rent district would be our development laboratory. With the right success we might even be able to move that. I would have settled for a money-losing operation for a year or two if we could have gotten off to a good start."

Entirely different purposes, entirely different goals—yet each felt they understood the other. Let's consider the second question of Situation Prevention.

2. Have I prepared the way for the successful completion of this action by establishing communications and coordination with those who will be affected?

Charlie concentrated on the manufacturing operation, and his staff selection shows that. The president wanted community relations first.

Why did the people reject the new plant? Why did the union have such an easy organizing job? Why didn't the bank president bend a little and provide the loans that were well within his authority?

All for the same reason—the Elf management ignored the town. They didn't become involved in community affairs as individuals. They sent the second team to the Rotary meetings. And most concrete of all, they brought an entire crew in from St. Louis to build the factory. Certainly an enlightened management would have insisted that the contractor use local labor for most of the job. It is all right to get an architect from another town. It is even permissible to require that the contractor be experienced; but manual labor, plumbing, masonry, and carpentry can certainly be contracted for in the local area. At least an effort can be made. Who can blame the people of Dalton for having their pride hurt? They retaliated by ignoring the new plant; thus the low attendance at the electronics school and the susceptibility to union organization.

Barry considered the "who" of this situation as being those people directly concerned with the day-to-day operation of the plant. He did not bother to try to know or understand the "thought leaders" of Dalton and quickly categorized their "culture" as farming. It is amazing what preconceptions can do to a person.

If he had been interested in involving the town in his purpose, he probably would have established an unofficial board of local leaders to advise him on the proper way to approach the community. It would not be necessary to accept their advice, and they would know that, but at least they would have been considered.

Since there was no cooperative effort discernible, the people naturally felt that the company had little interest in their welfare. The union representatives were smarter, so they offered to take such interest.

Thus, nothing came out the way it was supposed to.

Now, how about the third question of Situation Prevention?

3. Is the implementation method I have chosen the result of a thoughtful situation analysis, including "best" and "worst" anticipated results, or am I following normal practices?

Under Charlie Barry's plan, the best thing that could happen to him was to make a profit on schedule. But this is what is expected of a good manager anyway; therefore, there was little chance of being a hero by excelling. The worst result probably didn't enter his mind, but it is what happened. He chose a course that led him to be measured on one criterion only. As we know now, he ignored the other factors that the president was going to use to measure his success.

The three most important people on Barry's staff were the manufacturing manager, the public relations specialist, and the industrial relations director. Yet he chose proven, competent people in the first category only. He could have had anyone he wanted, but he *promoted* people—new people.

His implementation plan consisted entirely of a scheduled acquiring of inventory, people, and facilities. It did not take into consideration the effect on the community or the long-range goals of the corporation. He assumed that the corporate goals were unrealistic without finding out their intent.

Charlie Barry will go to his grave convinced that he was "had," and he may be correct in some of his feelings. But it was his responsibility to find out specifically, and in writing, what he was expected to accomplish. He didn't.

If you happen to be acquainted with a large corporation, you may find that it has several bright, experienced "staff assistants" who used to be executives and are now hunting for other "challenges." Some of them may have followed Charlie's path to this spot. Some of them may have gotten there by saying and implementing one of these statements:

1. "Don't give me any help. We'll straighten the situation out if corporate will leave us alone."
2. "I know the operation has been losing money for 2 years, but we are going to increase efficiency this year and will turn a profit."
3. "The way to turn this operation around is to cut out all the luxuries, so we're eliminating inspection, drawing control, and training."
4. "My people are too busy and our travel budget is too skimpy to participate in conferences and meetings."
5. "The customers don't understand."

It might be said that Charlie was dead when he took this assignment. He did not understand what the board wanted, and they didn't understand what he wanted. The fault must be equally shared, but since the organized world is constructed the way it is, the blame will fall on one head only. Anyone could predict whose head would be sacrificed.

It will do no good to pursue the thought that a deeper investigation of management intent must be conducted because it is not possible to go deep enough to unearth every possible desire. Even if you do this, the desires may change because of forces you could not foresee. Therefore, there are only two ways out:

1. Have an ironclad contract that spells out the objective specifically and the terms by which success or failure will be measured. (You have a very fat chance of getting this.)
2. Require constant involvement by those who will be judging.

If Charlie had had periodic meetings with top management to discuss his progress, his future planning, and the problems that existed, he would have become aware very soon that the board was interested in using this operation as a prototype for future expansion and vitally interested in community relationships.

If he hadn't known how to handle that, and it is permissible for a general manager to have a void or two in his competence, he could have asked for, and received, guidance and assistance.

In a nutshell, he got so wrapped up in the day-to-day jobs that he forgot to get other people involved. When the inevitable judgment day arrived, he had no sympathetic voice speaking for him at the head table It's as simple as that.

Consider the success record of those you have known who have accepted a difficult job only after insisting that they be left completely alone to work it out as they pleased. Even if the job came off right, they always suffered. Ever hear of Sir Walter Raleigh?

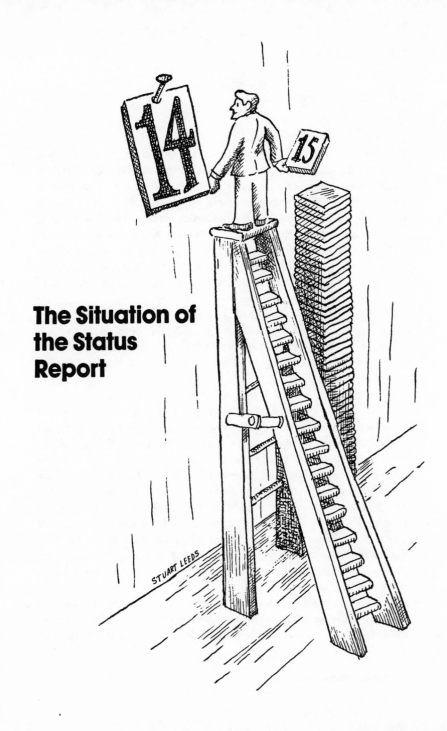

The Situation of
the Status
Report

STUART LEEDS

"Men are disturbed not by things, but by the
view which they take of things."
Epictetus

Problems exist and will continue to do so, regardless of your personal
wishes or drives. Relative seriousness has no bearing on their existence.
Problems exist because each human has a problem bucket that aches to
be filled. Where there are no problems, people will create some. Witness
the Garden of Eden; observe ancient Carthage; remember Edward Kent.

Who was Edward Kent? I don't know. His name was listed only to
permit you to observe yourself creating a problem for yourself. "Why
don't I know about Edward Kent when I know about Eden and Carthage?
Should I look it up? How can I have reached this age and never heard
of anyone obviously that famous?"

We seek problems. They rarely seek us. It is our duty as Situation
Managers to organize ourselves for the controlling of the daily problem
list that is anxiously scanned by those whose activities and attitudes are
important to us. Controlling, or at least understanding, this list is the Situation Manager's forte.

The first consideration is: How do we report a problem?

Those new to the Situation Management business may conceive that
a problem is a problem and that to report it is quite easy. You only list
the facts so that others may know what has happened, then act wisely
to overcome it. Unfortunately, the problem itself has little to do with how
people will react. They react independently of the situation itself and are
concerned only with making sure that their personal needs are achieved.
This is true regardless of the dedication and compassion residing within
their soul. The missionary is going to convert the cannibal, even if it
means being digested; the professional ball player is going to score, even
if it means causing his opponent to be fired, thus taking the bread from
the mouths of children; the mother will save her children, even if it means
wiping out half the town.

If we are to practice reporting a problem, we must consider it through
the mind of the person we want to impress, motivate, or mollify. Consider
the sinking of the Titanic. How would it look as seen through the eyes
of:

An environmentalist:

Ship Attacks Iceberg

In the early hours of today, the world's largest ship, coldly and without warning, viciously attacked Iceberg 23 who was floating along minding her own business. Twenty-three suffered a large gash in her port side, but courageously righted herself, shook off the ship, and proceeded bravely on her way. A protest has been filed with the British Ministry.

A maritime labor leader:

1800 Jobs Lost

Through the carelessness of the British Ministry, the Titanic has been permitted to ram an iceberg and sink. As a result, the Maritime Union has lost 1800 berths for its members. This is obviously a plot to ruin the union and make us beg for jobs. A protest has been filed with the British Ministry.

A merchant:

Woolens Ruined

Our spring showing will be delayed because the material being shipped from the British mills has been permitted to become waterlogged, as a result of the sinking of the Titanic. Because of this plot to drive woolen prices higher, we are considering purchasing our next order from New Zealand. A protest has been filed with the British Ministry.

The only purpose of reporting a problem is to create a desire for action on the part of those to whom you are reporting it. You must be able to gather together the right group of words if you are to achieve your purpose. You want something done and you want it done now! (Sometimes it is not necessary to mention the real problem.)

How would you report these situations in order to get action?

1. The boiler in your plant is well past retirement age. However, capital expenditures for replacement have been refused. Your engineer feels that it is going to expire in the next few days. If so, it will shut you down for several weeks because of the damage the failure will create. However, if you can obtain the money, you can put in a new one over the weekend.

2. A department store is continually dunning you to pay a bill that you do not owe. When contacted by telephone, they apologize for their

computer and assure you that everything will be all right next month. When next month rolls around, the computer threatens you with a visit from the sheriff.

3. Your daughter has decided to become a polo player.

When you report a problem, you want someone to do something which will result in eliminating the problem for you. Therefore, while sticking to facts, you must report the problem in the proper manner. For instance:

Problem No. 1

Q. Who needs to be influenced?

A. Top management.

Q. What concerns them most?

A. Loss of profits or presence of public sensation.

Q. What do I want?

A. A new boiler.

Combine the two and you have the following report:

MEMO

To: Top Management

From: Plant No. 6

We request approval of the attached emergency procedure. In the event of a predicted boiler explosion, we have arranged for civil defense personnel to assist with the injured. Production operations will be moved to the warehouse. It is felt that only 3 weeks of output will be lost and that we will be able to produce 45 percent of our regular commitment during that time period. We should be back on schedule 6 months after the explosion.

Problem No. 2

Q. Who needs to be influenced?

A. The department store's credit department.

Q. What concerns them most?

A. People paying their bills on time and the store's reputation.

Q. What do I want?

A. To have them bill me correctly and quit bothering me.

Combine the two and you have the following report:

MEMO

To: Credit Department

From: Citizens for Accurate Billing

We have selected your store as an example of computerized billing and are considering presenting you with our award of excellence. We plan to take a poll of your customers in the next few weeks. If we find no cases of duplicate or erroneous billing, you will be notified that you have won the award.

(Who says you can't set up a one-member committee?)

Problem No. 3

Q. Who needs to be influenced?

A. Your daughter.

Q. What concerns her most?

A. Her personal beauty and her urge for adventure.

Combine the two and you have the following report:

MEMO

To: Daughter

From: Father

Congratulations on deciding to take up polo instead of swimming. It is a fine sport. Not only is riding a horse excellent exercise, but it is broadening. Excuse my little joke. Love, Dad.

Now you may note that the subject has been slightly changed in each example. Therein lies the secret of proper problem reporting if you wish to excel as a Situation Manager. Problems are all in the way you look at them. The purpose of problem reporting is to get other people to look at problems the same way you do.

Let's see how one executive reported his problems:

"Let's look at the facts, old boy," said George Elmhurst to himself. "Just list the facts as they are, no shilly-shallying, no mishmash. Just give the bare basics and let the chips fall where they may."

MEMO

To: President, Friendly Corporation

From: George Elmhurst, General Manager,
Components Division

Subject: Quarterly Status Report

The overall situation in the division is very poor. We are 23 percent under budget in production output. Customers have returned 9 percent of the products shipped during the quarter because of poor quality. Sales orders are dropping every day, and it looks as if we will wind up under our sales budget by at least 30 percent. The union is very unhappy about projected layoffs, and their

leaders are talking about a strike to guarantee
job security. Also, we need a capital appropria-
tion of $123,540 to replace the plating facility.

I would appreciate some assistance from corporate staff.

"Oh boy," thought George, "I can see the old man going through the roof now. He won't even give me a chance to explain when he reads this letter. Most of it isn't my fault, or the fault of anyone here in the components division. Perhaps I'd better give this a good think."

Let us now proceed to an analysis of this situation according to the questions of Situation Prevention. We shall assume that George has voluntarily decided to do this himself. His motivation may be classed as one of sheer desperation.

SITUATION PREVENTION GUIDE

1. What are the short- and long-range purposes of this action? The short-range purpose is to fulfill the requirement of telling headquarters what is going on each quarter. The long-range purpose is to get some help in this impossible situation I have on my hands. The union is making its own rules, and the customers are getting the wrong idea of what our products are supposed to do for them.

2. Have I prepared the way for the successful completion of this action by establishing communications and coordination with those who will be affected?
Holy mackerel! I have never asked for headquarters' help up to now. In fact, I have ignored it.

But really, they are part of the problem. Perhaps
I should request a total evaluation, but that
might cause me problems too. The answer must be
that so far I have not prepared the way. I'd
better start preparing it. That means that I will
have to explain my problems in such a way as to
make them feel compassionate toward this division.

3. Is the implementation method I have chosen the result of a thoughtful situation analysis, including "best" and "worst" anticipated results, or am I following normal practices? I have not really thought about the
thing. I have merely followed the reports of my
staff. There are probably better ways of doing
things. If I send in the report as it was written, I'll be fired. If I suppress it, I'll be
fired. At this point, I think I'd better take a
look at this total situation and examine the problems one at a time.

While Mr. Elmhurst is wrestling with his next move, let's review the history of his experience at the components division of the Friendly Corporation.

George joined Friendly 3 years ago. He had been a plant general manager prior to that time and was looking for greater things in his career. At Friendly, he became assistant to the executive vice president for a year in order to learn about the corporation and, at the same time, provide some of his expertise to the components division. Components was a growing operation, but it was losing money. Friendly had decided to enter the field starting from scratch and had anticipated that it would take them 6 years to start receiving a return on their investment. At the end of 6 years, the division was still losing money and returning a minus 9 percent on sales. The tax-loss days were behind them, and something had to be done. The board debated the alternatives of getting out of the business altogether or trying one more time. Since the potential looked so favorable, they decided that they would purchase another company in the field, Flower, and merge it with their own components division. Their real target was the management of Flower and, in particular, the boy wonder of the components field, Harvey Harrison. Harvey had brought Flower from nothing to something in only 4 years.

The deal was consummated. The units were merged, and the struggle started anew. Harvey's business projection for the next 2 years indicated that the combined components operation would soon be pushing the big boys out of the field, and promised a break-even by the end of the first year and an 8 percent return at the end of the second. Everyone was pleased except George Elmhurst, who thought the plant overly ambitious. George recognized that he had anticipated being given responsibility for those divisions, so he quieted his fears by reminding himself that he was just jealous.

Harvey operated. He centralized the manufacturing operations, he moved sales to corporate in order to handle the broadened line more efficiently, and he cut the overhead. (George noted that most of the cuts were among the Friendly personnel and that the Flower people were pretty much in control of the operation.)

But it just wouldn't move.

At the end of the first year, Harvey threw up his hands ("to collect a large stock offer from another company," thought George) and resigned. George was thrust into the gap as division general manager and instructed to pull the job out of the hole. He applied all his skill, worked increasingly long hours, cultivated and developed his team, and, as a result, found himself facing the last quarter of the year predicting not an 8 percent return, but a 15 percent loss.

It is at this point that we join George preparing his quarterly report.

"I think I know all the problems," mused George, "but I'm not getting very far with the solution. Perhaps I should try to spell out the situation one line at a time by utilizing the Situation Management procedure."

SITUATION ANALYSIS GUIDE

Awareness

1. What seems to be the situation? This division is losing money. Hard work and desire have not changed that fact. I am faced with reporting personal failure to headquarters; yet in my heart I feel that we have done everything that could be done under the present plan.

2. How did I find out that the situation exists?
The cost figures are accurate. I know that, because we just revised the accounting procedure 3 months ago. That's when I discovered that we were being too kind to ourselves in the inventory and capital areas. Of course, the place has been losing money all along.

3. What is the potential effect of this matter?
For me it could mean the end of a fine relationship. For the division--disaster. For the corporation--a loss of face and capital.

4. How serious is it? Very serious. I think this may be the end of the road.

5. How much time do I have to extricate myself?
About 1 week. That's when the report is due at headquarters.

Evaluation

1. What evidence leads me to believe that the situation exists? Performance data: reports of sales, schedules, product quality, and costs.

2. What is the specific source of this evidence?
It comes from the controller's office, quality control, and the sales department.

3. Do I know whether the evidence is factual?
I have checked it out in sufficient detail to know that it is an accurate portrayal of our situation.

4. Can I list the steps that created the situation?
Yes, but I don't think anyone will like it. We tried to be born whole, producing a complete line. We didn't have the established customers and had to sell on price, while promising product performance in excess of our competitors. To achieve

this, we attempted to motivate our people to perform impossible tasks and bought the skills to do
so. We have tried to purchase success.

5. Whose mind must I change to resolve the problem?
The president and the board.

6. What does that mind think now?   They think that
the only thing missing in this operation is hard
work and time. They also think the time has run
out and it may need some harder workers.

7. How will I know when the situation is resolved?
When the division starts returning a profit and
the board thinks I am the greatest.

Action

1. Relate the key individuals to the key issues.
The board feels that the failure of this division
to be successful is the result of poor management
on my part.

2. Why do they believe this?   Because the success
plan was created by a man with a long history of

achievement, and, in addition, the board created

the operating policy.

3. What would it require to separate them from this belief? They have to be shown factually that the

approach we are using cannot possibly succeed, and

they have to be offered a foolproof plan that will

sell components.

4. What is the best method to use in this separation?
We need to review the whole operation, determine

a different strategy, and realign ourselves to im-

plement it.

5. How do I implement the method? I would have

to obtain the board's attention long enough to

make the presentation without being fired and then

get them to participate long enough to become part

of the solution. Really, I think all we need to

do is cut our catalog down to where we are

peddling the things that are selling anyway and

drop the loss items.

6. Once it is over, what steps do I take to ensure that it will never happen again?   I promise that I will

never take over an operation unless I am able to

create the performance plan myself.

At this point, our hero took pen in hand once more and addressed his report to the president of Friendly.

MEMO

To: President, Friendly Corporation

From: George Elmhurst, General Manager,
Components Division

Subject: Quarterly Status Report

1. You know from the weekly reports that we are falling behind on sales and output. In addition, our warranty costs are 9 percent of sales, inventory is over budget by 18 percent, and the union is threatening to strike.

2. I have verified all of these items. In my opinion, they will become a more serious problem during the next quarter unless we take some drastic action.

3. These problems are only symptoms of the deeper situation involving us. Our real problems are:

a. Our product line is too wide. I am attaching a list of money losers that I recommend we cut out tomorrow. I know that sales will say they must have a full line to obtain orders, but we are just going to have to decide that this is no longer true.

b. We have patterned our specifications and our processes after our competitors' products. We must develop some proprietary products.

c. Our quality problems will go away when we start delivering what we know we have, but I feel we must investigate the customers' requirements in more detail and test to the same methods they use.

d. We must tell the union that if they will not go along with us on cutting back the work force in order to meet these commitments, we will close the plant -- and mean it.

4. If we are not willing to do these things, I recommend going out of the components business.

5. A change of management will not alter the facts now before us. "New blood" will only create new promises until they begin to comprehend the situation it has taken me 9 months to understand.

6. If you are agreeable to these moves, I request that you provide me with a corporate staff task team consisting of industrial engineers, reliability and quality control people, marketing survey personnel, and an inventory specialist. I will need them for 2 months. If I am correct, we will break even in 6 months and turn our first profit, a modest 1 percent, in 8 months.

7. If you do not feel that you can accept these action recommendations, I would appreciate the opportunity to transfer to another position within the corporation. If that is not possible, then I shall resign at your request.

Respectfully,

George Elmhurst

"Now," thought George, "that ought to spell it out clearly enough. After reading it over, I think I'll remove the 'Respectfully'; even the old man would think that was laying it on a little thick. Let's see how this solution would work out."

SITUATION PREVENTION GUIDE

1.   What are the short- and long-range purposes of this action?   The short-range purpose is to get myself some time to do the things that I now know must be done. The long-range purpose is to actually get this operation making money.

2.   Have I prepared the way for the successful completion of this action by establishing communications and coordination with those who will be affected?
I've started it. There is no use going to the union or the staff people until I've been told by the president whether or not my ideas are accept-able. However, in order to make sure that at least some communication is achieved, I think I will deliver this report in person instead of mailing it. The president doesn't like division managers to leave their operations. Seeing me there will add emphasis to the seriousness of this matter.

3. Is the implementation method I have chosen the result of a thoughtful situation analysis, including "best" and "worst" anticipated results, or am I following normal practices?   I think I have done a proper analysis

on this one. It would be possible to "phony" the

thing along for another quarter or two until I

found myself another job, but this has to be the

best way -- face up to the problem and fight it.

The best thing that can happen is that

they go along with me and we are successful. The

worst thing is that I get fired. No, wait a min-

ute, the really worst thing is that I get fired

and someone else comes in, operates to the old

plan, and makes money. Can that happen? No, I

don't believe it can.

George took his plan to headquarters. To his surprise, the president listened carefully, interrogated incisively, and then—agreed. George went back to work and 8 months later returned a profit of 1.8 percent.

He often wondered what made this all come about. There are several possible solutions. Perhaps the president was waiting all this time for someone to create a new plan. Perhaps George could only make something work that he invented. Perhaps his plan was the only way. I will let the reader decide. The important aspect is that George evaluated his situation properly, took action, knew where he was going, and went there.

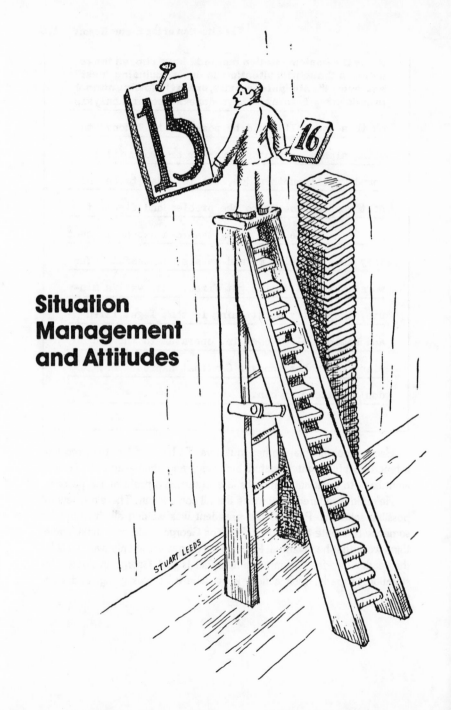

**Situation
Management
and Attitudes**

STUART LEEDS

It is a constant source of amazement to me that many things we know or think we know turn out to be wrong in some way. Not just little things; big things also.

Columbus was wrong: he went on his trip because he thought the world was about 18,000 miles around. That meant he could pack enough provisions in his little boats to make it all the way to China. The Portugese, and the ancient Greeks for that matter, knew that the earth was 25,000 miles in circumference—too great a distance to attempt to travel. That is why the Portugese, who were the great navigators of that day, didn't get to America first. Sometimes you can know too much.

So Columbus went off to starve to death in the mid-Pacific as they all chortled. However, he ran into a brand new world and thus changed from confused explorer to master strategist by the simple expedient of coming home instead of disappearing.

All those stories about the educated people thinking you would fall off if you sailed out to the horizon were not true. There is also some question of the authenticity of the story about Queen Isabella and her jewels. It is suspected that Columbus received much of his financing from the Moors and the Hebrews, who had until the end of 1492 to convert or leave Spain. Since they had both been there over 900 years (more than twice the number of years since America was discovered), they really had no place to go.

On another subject concerning things we believe that may not be accurate:

Take a group of men, not by their own will, lock them in a metal container for months under strict discipline and what do you get? Hate? Rape? Terror? Ganging up? All those bad things?

Not necessarily. The Navy stacked its draftees together, elbow to elbow, for months. Most cases involved no sight or even smell of the enemy. Dull, drab, boring days followed by more of the same. Yet the Navy has traditionally had no problem of the sailors terrorizing each other. And mutiny is something only for the movies.

But state prisons, boy, do they have the problems! They take people, place them in similar conditions, and what do they get? You know; the newspapers and literature are full of it. Dehumanizing, degrading "animals" preying on each other.

What is the big difference? The people are much the same. The modern state prison and the modern naval vessel have a great deal in common concerning living space, entertainment, food, educational programs, and so forth. Nuclear vessels don't even come to the surface for months.

In my opinion, guards and prison administrators create much of the problem. They feel they are put there to punish the prisoners and, for the most part they dislike them, particularly those of the minority races. Certainly there are a few guards who should be made saints for their feelings and their work. But for the overwhelming majority, it is their role in life to punish. And they seem to enjoy it.

When New York state prison guards went on strike in 1979, the governor called out the National Guard. For 16 days, nervous untrained guardsmen stood by outside while the supervisors and the inmates ran the prisons. There was not a single case of rape, assault, or even something requiring disciplinary action in any of New York's twenty-eight prisons. Not one.

Take the same idea and apply it to the schools that are having strife between teachers and students. There is a new breed of student in the land, and you can make a sound case about not making everyone stay in school until the age of 16. There are many causes for disruptions.

But the biggest change I see is in the attitude of the teachers, attitudes that show that teaching, for many of them, is no longer a noble profession; it is a source of security, and its sole purpose is to provide a living.

I can't knock anyone who works for a living; that isn't what I mean. Teachers have always had a difficult job and certainly should be well paid. However, we have a nation under constant criticism because its children can't read, write, or handle the normal tasks of basic education. We hear that 25 percent of our people are functionally illiterate; we hear that people are graduating from high school without being able to read.

And yet, at the same time, we see more and more bright students becoming lawyers, physicians, and scientists, with all sorts of advanced educational achievements. These are fine young people, well oriented and necessary to the nation's growth.

But it is beginning to appear that only the well-behaved and the well-oriented get taught. Is that the way it is supposed to be? Or is it the job of the teacher to teach everyone?

The problem is that the educators think they are in some other business. They think they are building systems, not training individuals. Systems are designed so that the super-bright and the super-dumb get no satisfaction. All systems work that way.

And remember—education is the third largest industry in the United States, right after food and construction. We spend over $200 billion a year on education at all levels. So it is not a lack of money. We need more education of the educators. For instance, it has just come to light that the size of the class has little to do with the amount students will learn. How about that?

Welfare

If you are an ordinary, well-read American, you may think that most of the welfare money goes to inner-city blacks. A lot of money goes there, mostly to children or single-parent families. But the majority of welfare money goes to rural whites.

Organization

It would be hard to find a subject, particularly in the field of management, that has had more written about it than organization. That is because the possibility of shifting people around in order to solve problems is something that is really interesting to all of us. Particularly if we are the shifter and not the shiftee.

If you ask any functional manager, any one at all, to whom that particular function should be reported, you will receive one answer only: the function is so important that it must be reported to the chief executive officer (CEO). Otherwise, the manager will predict, the job will not get done.

If you look at the typical corporation chart, you will see that the functions being reported to the CEO are something like this: administration; controller; treasurer; public relations; legal; and the president who handles all the operations.

The ones fighting for some attention and support are purchasing, quality, production control, consumer affairs, design, marketing, and similar activities. And these are very important functions that face a tough life. They need all the help they can get.

So how come all the operations reporting to the CEO's office are the ones that don't need any help? They are all perfectly capable of getting along with very little direction. The controller follows accepted accounting practices and never goes to the CEO asking which part of the page to fill out.

Legal tells the boss what to get involved in and what to stay away from. Public relations asks only for approval of their budget, never for advice, although they will accept suggestions. The treasurer deals with banks and financial analysts; once in a while this person talks with the boss about borrowing or paying back some money. But there is very little day-to-day activity.

Now what is it that kills a company? It is bad quality, overpaying subcontractors and suppliers, product safety suits, sloppy marketing, or inadequate design that does you in.

All I am saying is that the CEO traditionally takes to breast those things which require very little of him or her, those things for which existence is assured by the requirements of the function. Avoided are those things which really need some help and guidance.

Over the years, an attitude has developed that says power comes only from the office of the CEO. Thus, those who report there have power and those who don't, don't. This creates a super-elite whose only purpose is to retain that power.

You could put them all on the rack and they would never admit that the lower functions, reporting down the line, weren't just as important as their own. They probably truly believe that. However, if you asked them if they personally were more important, they could only admit (being honest souls) that to tell the truth they were.

Below the power level, the function is everything. Above that level, the individual is everything. Thus the CEO, wanting to talk to the purchasing director, might say: "Ask the purchasing director, Joe Swithers, to come up to the office, please."

However, should the controller be the desired attendee, the command will be: "Ask Ethyl to stick her head in, please." CEOs are always polite.

Thus an attitude is born, nurtured, and encouraged. Yet no one admits to it. The CEO who would like to reduce the amount of direct reports should have a long hard think about the attitudes involved. My recommendation is that the weakest functions should report to the top until they are strong. Then shift them around. Thus shall the weak inherit the better offices.

Healing

The electronic revolution has brought faith healing out of the tent and into the home. People everywhere are laying hands on each other with sometimes amazing results. I personally believe strongly in healing, and I consider myself a born-again Christian in the fullest meaning. Healing is something we should all take seriously and practice with dedication.

However, I think it is all directed at the wrong place. People are forever working on physical healing. And certainly the affected individual, myself on several occasions, can think of little else besides the hope that some pain or discomfort will leave the body. I praise the Lord for any physical healing that takes place.

But the limp that disappears will have little effect on the social, economic, or political life of our world. It is important to that person and his or her family; for them it is good and should be.

But the healing that needs to take place in the world today is concerned with attitudes. People still tend to place others into categories or groups. Then they hate, tolerate, accept, or love these groups depending on their own personal attitudes. The characteristics that create attitudes have at least two things in common: they are usually incorrect and they are always emotional.

The history of the world is stained by one group of the same nation quarreling with another. The black and white misunderstanding has held the United States captive longer than any other single problem of the nation. Even today, these two groups of warm, loving people still don't know each other, still distrust on sight, and have not learned to accept one another as plain old people. It is heartbreaking.

Somewhere in this continual confrontation, which has now gone underground, is an orientation of racial fear and blind distrust. In a couple of generations it will perhaps disappear, but not until people actually begin living in common, forgetting color or national origin, and accepting others as the individuals they are. If they are rotten, then they are rotten. If good, then good. But it is because of themselves, not because of their color or name.

If you read the history of any European nation, you will find that the civil wars were always between the north and south. Even today in Germany, for instance, the Berliners and Swabians snicker at each other's behavior patterns. How come the wars weren't between east and west?

There is an interesting pattern that can be seen in the states in this country as well as on a national basis. Individual states have their industrial centers in the north and the rural areas in the south. Yet if you move south to the next state, they have the same arrangement. Strange.

And look at Europe. North of France: industrial, brisk. South of France: wine, cheese, sun. Then go a little more south and you come to the north of Spain. There you see: industrial, brisk. Drop to the south of Spain and presto: wine, cheese, and sun. The behavior patterns of the people have changed over the last few years, but they are identifiable.

At any rate, you will find that people have these preconceived notions about each other. They wind up in jokes, in conversation, and in attitudes that make it impossible for many people to communicate with each other. Many people are so impressed with the role assigned to them that they continually act it out, thus perpetuating the myths.

We could make a lot more progress if we were to concentrate on healing our attitudes. If we would put more emphasis on this, then we might wind up cleansed of the hate that holds us back.

Now you may think all of this has nothing to do with the management of situations. But it has a great deal to contribute. The biggest single problem facing industry today, both blue and white collar, is low productivity. The biggest advantage the Japanese have over the western nations is high productivity.

The Japanese are a homogeneous group. With the exception of a tiny minority of slightly larger "white" Japanese, they are all very much the same. They all came from Japan.

In the United States, we have people from every nation of the world poured together in one big melting pot that didn't melt all of the original national characteristics out of us. So while Japanese workers pay virtually no attention to the person beside them, American workers must concentrate on classifying their co-workers. Does this one belong to the lazy, money-mad, sloppy, dumb, or whichever categories we all know about? At least we think we know about them, which is worse.

So while we all have our little wars going on, filled with mistrust and lowered effort, the Japanese are merrily beating our economic brains out. And if you think that is bad, wait another generation till the Chinese get organized.

When you don't have to worry so much about what people think about you before they even know you, and when you don't have to spend time thinking about the person working with you, it is possible to work harder and be more productive. When attitudes are healed, and hatred is not automatic, success has a better chance.

The smart Situation Manager will take all this to heart when installing programs in a company. Those communication efforts constructed with all of this in mind will succeed beyond your wildest anticipation.

People yearn for the chance to be a community, to work together in harmony and purpose. Companies seem to go out of their way to make this difficult. The old concept of management was to keep the employees from banding together for any reason. But today a few companies are learning.

It sounds like an oversimplification, but if you can arrange for people to understand what it is they are supposed to do, encourage them to do it, recognize their achievements, and pay a little attention to them in between times—that's all there is to it. In the process they will forget their intramural quarrels.

I will always remember what Mayor Evers of Fayette, Mississippi, said about this: "When everyone is involved, they don't have time to run around with white sheets over their heads."

Beware the "I's" of Situation Management

STUART LEEDS

"And every star and every whirling planet,
And every constellation in the sky,
Revolves around the center of the universe:
That lovely thing called I."

Oscar Hammerstein

The problem most of us face when starting to use Situation Management is that we forget that not only are we ourselves part of the situation, but more likely we have contributed a great deal to its existence. It takes at least two for a conflict.

In order to overcome this natural tendency, we must look very honestly at each situation to assess our personal contribution to its existence.

If you remember, "The Situation of the Boss versus Peace and Quiet" (Chapter 5), Harriet, our hero, helped cause the situation by forgetting to keep in touch with her counterparts. Tom Johnson, in "The Situation of the Unwanted Improvement" (Chapter 10), helped cause his problem by taking his eye off the doughnut while detailing the dimensions of the hole in infinite detail. It can happen to anyone.

Some years ago I was quality manager of a missile program. One of my areas of responsibility was the inspection and test of the missiles before they were sent to the test range for firing. To conduct these tests, as well as other ones, I had a very large department, the latest in special and complex equipment, competent people, and the absolute support and encouragement of the company's management.

When the "birds" would arrive at the test range, they would be checked out by the customer's people, as well as engineers from our own company. Each report that the test range filed listed some errors. They would consistently find six or seven things wrong with the missile. These varied all the way from a plant scratch to an uncaged gyro.

But considering the complexity of the system (it must have had at least 50,000 parts), I wasn't too concerned. We seemed to be getting better each time, and I knew for sure that our faults were a lot less numerous than those of other programs. However, the customer kept getting more upset, and soon my own management was snapping at me.

I kept explaining the laws of probability, showing improvement curves, and in general trying to get them to understand that they couldn't expect things to get much better as long as mere people were involved.

But the pressure continued, and signs began to appear that perhaps

I should worry about Law 1. And in spite of myself, I sat down to give the thing a good think. "Why are these people being so unreasonable?"

Obviously, they had not had the experience with the aspects of quality evaluation that I had. Just as obviously, they were not going to let me stay around long enough to teach them this experience. There had to be a way out.

Up to that time, I had assumed that I was not part of the problem, or that if I were, it was only because I had failed to educate my leaders properly. Then it occurred to me that I was very happy with six or seven defects per bird and that perhaps my people recognized this. They were apparently meeting my standard. They also weren't upset.

Therefore, I called all the supervisors together and told them that from now on our standard was no defects. "Zero Defects" is what I wrote on the board. They argued for a few moments, shrugged, and went back to work. Two deliveries later, the people at the test range could find nothing wrong with the missile and told us so. After that, zero defects became routine. Once in a while, something would slip through. Everyone would raise Cain, and we would get back to doing the job right.

Now, it is apparent that we had proved that a dedicated crew of competent people with the proper equipment could find all the defects or problems in a system. However, that is very expensive. What we needed was a way of preventing the problems from occurring in the first place. Thus, working on the basis that the problem is the standards of management (the product looks like the manager), and not the work standards of the people, I constructed the concept of Zero Defects for the purpose of preventing defects.

The concept goes like this:

"The products of industry are not good enough, customer complaints are rising, and there is too much waste. Those products that work trouble-free do so because of an investment in test, inspection, and service that is out of proportion. Many companies spend 10, 15, and even 20 percent of their sales dollar on scrap, rework, warranty, service, test, and inspection. The errors that produce this waste are caused directly by the personnel of the plant, both employees and management.

"To eliminate this waste, to improve the operation, to become more efficient, we must concentrate on preventing the defects and errors that plague us. The defect that is prevented doesn't need repair, examination, or explanation.

"The first step is to examine and adopt the attitude of defect prevention. This attitude is called, symbolically, Zero Defects.

"Zero Defects is a standard for management, a standard that management can convey to the employees to help them to decide to do the job right the first time.

"People are conditioned to believe that error is inevitable. We not only accept error, we anticipate it. Whether we are designing circuits, planning a project, soldering joints, typing letters, completing an account ledger, or assembling components, it does not bother us to make a few errors—and management plans for these errors to occur. We feel that human beings have a built-in error factor.

"However, we do not maintain the same standard when it comes to our personal life. If we did, we would resign ourselves to being short-changed now and then as we cash our paychecks. We would expect hospital nurses to drop a certain percent of all newborn babies. We would expect to go home to the wrong house by mistake periodically. As individuals, we do not tolerate these things. Thus we have a double-standard—one for ourselves, one for the company.

"The reason for this is that the family creates a higher performance standard for us than the company does.

"In short, we must determine if we as managers have made our desires clear to those who look to us for guidance and direction. We must provide an understandable, constant standard for quality performance.

"Consider the three basic areas of performance in any organization: cost, schedule, and quality.

"All of these are vital for success. Each requires the establishment of a performance standard that cannot be misunderstood.

"Take cost. Everyone understands what $2.34 looks like. There may be some argument about what to do with money, but everyone understands its substance. A budget is set and the standard is to make the job and the funds come out together.

"Schedule also has an understandable common base: time. We all use the same standard calendars and clocks. Delivery and completion dates are specified in contracts and requirements. We either meet the dates or we do not.

"Now what is the existing standard for quality?

"Most people talk about an acceptable quality level (AQL). An AQL really means a commitment before we start the job to produce imperfect material. Let me repeat: An acceptable quality level is a commitment before we start the job that we will produce imperfect material. An AQL, therefore, is not a management standard. It is a determination of the status quo. Instead of the managers setting the standard, the operation sets the standard.

"Consider the AQL you would establish on the product you buy. Would you accept an automobile that you knew in advance was 15 percent defective? 5 percent? 1 percent? One half of 1 percent? How about the nurses that care for newborn babies? Would an AQL of 3 percent on mishandling be too rigid?

"The Zero Defects concept is based on the fact that mistakes are caused by two things: lack of knowledge and lack of attention.

"Lack of knowledge can be measured and attacked by tried and true means. But lack of attention is a state of mind. It is an attitude problem that must be changed by the person involved. When presented with the challenge to do this and the encouragement to attempt it, the individual will respond enthusiastically. Remember—Zero Defects is not a motivation method; it is a performance standard. And it is not just for production people; it is for everyone. Some of the biggest gains occur in the nonproduction areas.

"The Zero Defects program must be personally directed by top management.

"People receive their standards from their leaders. They perform to the requirements given to them. They must be told that your personal standard is Zero Defects.

"To gain the benefits of Zero Defects, you must decide to make a personal commitment to have improvement in your operation. You must want it.

"The first step is: Make the attitude of Zero Defects your personal standard."

Now that seemed clear to me. However, I found people thinking that Zero Defects was a worker motivation program and blaming all the problems on the workers. For years I have made speeches and written articles saying that it isn't worker motivation, saying that management is the bad guy, and trying to have the quality management professionals recognize that we are dealing with a new management philosophy, not a propaganda program. To no avail.

The fact that Zero Defects has succeeded so well over the years is due to the intelligence of the workers who took it for what it is supposed to be. How did I fail in explaining it? I assumed that everyone had gone through the same emotional experience I did. The thinking will be corrected some day, but it won't be because I did the job right the first time.

When you analyze a problem through the use of the Situation Analysis Guide, always use the Situation Prevention Guide as a check on yourself to make sure that in your eagerness to express your brilliant solution, you have not overlooked something.

Another of the problems of getting people to take Situation Management seriously is this: they feel they don't need it. After all, if you are employed in a significant position, are adequately pampered by company, family, and staff, and can point with pride to a successful fight to attain your present position—well, it is tough to argue with you.

And, of course, those who have achieved some recognized success can look back to the tough old days and identify other strivers who didn't make it. Some even recount modestly a few of the things they have done in order to make life a little more bearable for those unfortunates.

But life isn't what you did before; life is what you are doing now. All things are relative in terms of your current skill in handling things.

Did you ever notice that some people always succeeded when they were youngsters? They were the ones selected for all of the honor and attention. Many of those youthful stars lost their glitter when they passed 30 or so. Suddenly they were unable to be super-winners anymore. Everything changed.

What changed was they hadn't altered their success plan. They were still doing the same old things. In their case it was pleasing adults. Once you learn how to please adults, you have it made as a kid. However, when you become the adult, it just doesn't work as well.

So all of us must pay attention to how we are doing now. We must not rely on the programs and techniques of the past. Doing over what you've done before only lasts so long. Every time you do something again, more and more personal action is involved. You have to do more to drag it through each time.

Therefore, the executive, who is supposed to grow into a life of ease and delegation, finds that more work is required than ever before. The thoughts of utilizing Situation Management concepts are attractive, but must be postponed until time is available. Of course it never is, or will be.

In fact, the executive is often heard to suggest that a course on such things should be scheduled for the lower levels of the organization. If they were doing their jobs, the executive would have plenty of time to learn how to have plenty of time. Or something like that.

The executive gets paid for doing the job and feels like a pro. In fact, that may be the proudest term of reference heard from those busy lips.

But what are the characteristics of a professional?

The pro wins no matter what. The pro is in control of personal skills, in command of time, gets the required results with a minimum of extra effort. Setbacks occur occasionally, but are viewed merely as a source of reeducation.

The pro is relaxed, confident, poised, aware of everything happening within any situation. Strikes are made when the iron is precisely the correct temperature, and only then. The moment to move is chosen thoughtfully; there is no wasted motion.

The presence of wasted motion identifies the nonpro quickly. If you are not in control, then you must participate in everything happening to make certain you are not left out. If you throw enough balls at the hoop, you are going to sink one now and then. The nonpro works long on things not personally chosen and is involved with activities that are not considered too important, but that is the style that goes with the role.

One good example of the difference between pro and nonpro is setting objectives. There are really only two types of objectives: personal and business. Pros are specific; nonpros are vague and their objectives are unmeasurable.

Nonpro: "I want my children to have a good education."

    Pro: "I will set aside 10 percent of my income in order to build an education fund for my children."

Nonpro: "I will do my part in improving our social conditions."

    Pro: "I will head up the Salvation Army fund drive and collect $1 million for them."

Every goal doesn't have to have a number for dollars in it, but it must have some measurable characteristic. Doing well is not all that measurable. Pros deal in the measurable; nonpros in the subjective.

You may never be a professional athlete; there are only about 3000 of them in the United States. It would seem that a lot more are around, but if you count only those who earn their living through excellence in their sport, that is about right.

How many pros do you suppose there are in your field or in your company or in your office or in your home? One way to tell is by listening to the goals. Do they say things like: "Improve customer relations"? A nonpro objective.

"Reduce customer complaints by 23 percent in 12 months," "reduce operating costs by 4.5 percent of sales while maintaining present output," "get three As and two Bs during the next term," "raise productivity from 86 to 94 percent by the first of July." All pro objectives.

How would people rate you if they saw only your goals displayed?

Situations to Practice Prevention By

STUART LEEDS

Situation 1

You have been given the job of establishing standard operating procedures in the 57 regional offices of your company. You have no staff other than a secretary you share with another manager. You decide to write operating procedures, issue them, and then conduct a series of seminars so that all the area office managers can learn how to comply with the procedures.

Use the Situation Prevention Guide to see how you are going to make out.

Situation 2

You have been appointed to the board of regents of your alma mater, a private school. The Student Committee for Academic Freedom has just submitted a petition to the board, requesting the right to participate in the annual performance review of faculty members. The faculty is up in arms at this request. The board has asked you to talk with the representatives of each group and develop a solution. You listen to both stories, decide that the students have a case, and recommend that they be permitted to participate.

Use the Situation Prevention Guide to see how you are going to make out.

Situation 3

You receive a letter from the Internal Revenue Service telling you that they have decided to audit your tax form. The only item you can think of that they might question is your practice of deducting one room in the house as an office. Therefore, you invite the agent to do the auditing at your house so that you can offer the use of your desk and adding machine.

Use the Situation Prevention Guide to see how you are going to make out.

Situation 4

Business is somewhat less than sensational. It is apparent that severe cutbacks will have to be made. You are assigned the task. After reviewing the budget situation, you recommend a 15 percent cut across the board. Every department is told to cut 15 percent immediately. Your cost reduction goal is met. Was this a good decision?

Situations 1 and 4 are discussed in detail on the following pages. Situations 2 and 3 are up to you.

Situation 1

To establish common operating procedures in 57 regional offices, you write and distribute them and plan seminars to teach their compliance.

SITUATION PREVENTION GUIDE

1. What are the short- and long-range purposes of this action? The short-range purpose is to establish a set of operating procedures that will fit all of the offices, and get the office managers to start using them. The long-range purpose is to have the procedures proved very successful in terms of cost savings and efficiency so that I can get recognition and be promoted to a better job.

2. Have I prepared the way for the successful completion of this action by establishing communications and coordination with those who will be affected?
I have done half of it. That is, my boss knows

about it because that's where the assignment came
from.   When I start having the seminars on the
procedures, the office managers will know about
it.   However, they won't have anything to say
about the content of the procedures or the way
they are to be implemented.   They will come in
cold--that might not be too good.

3.   Is the implementation method I have chosen the result of a thoughtful situation analysis, including "best" and "worst" anticipated results, or am I following normal practices?   Guilty.   I have just picked out a traditional method, actually like the type used by an
army.   The best thing that could happen would be
that they would accept and use the procedures I
have developed.   The worst thing would be that the
procedures wouldn't be adequate and would cause
more problems than we now have.   Another worst
could be that they would feel left out and would
not participate at all (Laws 2, 4, and 6).

4.   How am I going to make out?   Not very well.
I better do a Situation Analysis on this.

SITUATION ANALYSIS GUIDE

Awareness

1. What seems to be the situation?   I am about to write up a bunch of procedures to be used by all our office managers. I'm not sure that the procedures will be adequate or that the managers will even use them.

2. How did I find out that the situation exists?
I didn't really. However, I used to be an office manager, and I don't feel I would like being handled in the way I was going to do it.

3. What is the potential effect of this matter?
If I don't get the cooperation of the office managers, then the whole bit is dead, including me.

4. How serious is it?   Critical.

5. How much time do I have to extricate myself?
A lot of time. I didn't start anything yet, so there is nothing to undo. I have time to get smart, perhaps 6 or 7 months.

Evaluation

1. What evidence leads me to believe that the situation exists? My own personal experience, plus Laws of Situation Management 2, 4, and 6.

2. What is the specific source of this evidence?
When I was an office manager, I resented receiving any direction from headquarters. Also, it is apparent that since none of the 57 managers involved are demanding that all offices operate alike, they haven't thought much about it. This program is not exactly the people's choice.

3. Do I know whether the evidence is factual?
I think I'm going to have to take a trip around the company to make sure. However, my own past experience is certainly factual, and I have seen enough to believe that the laws are true.

4. Can I list the steps that created the situation?
I guess it started when I just pulled a traditional solution out of my drawer without thinking about the particular situation we have here.

5.   Whose mind must I change to resolve the problem?
Mine is already changed. That leaves the 57

office managers.

6.   What does that mind think now?   I'm going to

have to go see for sure, but it seems to me that

they probably think things are all right now and

that they don't need to have a new set of proce-

dures for the purpose of coordinating something

that they do not feel is a problem.

7.   How will I know when the situation is resolved?
When all the necessary procedures and disciplines

have been developed and are implemented by happy

managers.

Action

1.   Relate the key individuals to the key issues.
Our office managers don't see a need for unified

procedures, but my boss does. I have to figure a

way of having the procedures developed and imple-

mented.

2.   Why do they believe this?   The office managers

only see their own operations. They really think

the other operations don't have any effect on

them. My boss sees the whole operation and knows

differently.

3. What would it require to separate them from this belief?   Getting the office managers to talk with

each other about their problems.

4. What is the best method to use in this separation?
Bringing some of them together so that they can

learn that their problems are similar, and gener-

ating in them the desire to help each other.

5. How do I implement the method?   If I picked

several of the biggest offices, brought their

managers together for a meeting, and handled it

right, they might get the idea of inviting the

rest to join in a common effort. I should pre-

pare a presentation showing them the results, in

dollars, of not having common procedures and

practices.

6. Once it is over, what steps do I take to ensure that it will never happen again?   Keep the communications

going by making sure that the organization be-

comes formalized.

Epilogue

After thinking this out, our hero did indeed invite several key office managers to get involved. It also showed them that he didn't know how to resolve it. They appointed some study teams, asked the other managers to join them for an organizational meeting, and identified the necessary procedures. Using their headquarters' leader as a coordinator (and banner bearer), they attacked the problem of developing and implementing the procedures. Since the offices themselves were involved, the new procedures were accepted easily.

Obviously this took some time and a great deal of Situation Management. But it is doubtful that it could have been done by any other manner. It is well known that the mere making and issuing of procedures from headquarters has little to do with their use. This way everyone participated. Everyone got some credit, and the procedures themselves probably were better than one person could have developed anyway.

Situation 4

Cutbacks are necessary. You order an across-the-board 15% reduction.

SITUATION PREVENTION GUIDE

1. What are the short- and long-range purposes of this action? The short-range purpose is to reduce our expenditures immediately so the company will not suffer a loss. The long-range purpose is to permit us to ride out this recession period and come back strong when things improve.

2. Have I prepared the way for the successful completion of this action by establishing communications and coordination with those who will be affected?
No. I didn't even talk with anyone about it.

---

3. Is the implementation method I have chosen the result of a thoughtful situation analysis, including "best" and "worst" anticipated results, or am I following normal practices? There wasn't time to do all of that.

The mission had to be accomplished right now,

regardless of the immediate results. Perhaps

we can fix it later.

Epilogue

What this person needed was an understanding of the attitude of cost elimination. She forgot all about people being more important than things or people needing to participate in actions.

If your company is making 5 percent after taxes, you must have a $20 increase in sales in order to show a $1 increase in net profit. If you can determine a way not to spend $2, without hurting the operation, you will achieve the same result.

The problem, of course, is to determine which $2 not to spend. You do not want to reduce your capability of properly managing the business or cause your people to become so confined in their thinking that they miss opportunities.

Anyone can reduce costs. A few strokes of the pen and the sales department is eliminated or the factory is subleased or clerks are rationed on a per-square-foot basis. Nothing to it.

Unfortunately, much cost elimination is accomplished in just such an emotional or sporadic way. We all know of companies that initiate huge layoffs only to find, in a little while, that they must rehire and retrain.

Cost elimination is an attitude, and one that can be learned.

The essence of cost elimination is this: Managers are career-trained and oriented to a growing operation and growing economy. When a company and/or the economy gets in trouble, the manager must shift from this conventional style and enter the foreign world of doing things more cheaply. In conventional wisdom, cost elimination is a random thing forced by an oppressive environment, rather than a creative function exercised as part of a management concept.

This is always painful, undignified, and traumatic. No one ever forgets his or her personal experience in such an event. Constructive programs have to be junked. Valuable personnel must be eliminated. The whole operation is deliberately cut back, knowing that the road to recovery may be a long one. Top executives mutter about overexpansion, collapsing markets, and perhaps federal control. There is confusion in the executive ranks.

The facts of life are that the company did not keep cost elimination as a basic part of its management program. Suggestion programs, value analysis efforts, work effectiveness, and the like are assuredly conducted as a routine part of doing business. However, the overexpansion, the overorganization, and the neglect of expenses did not originate with the people who contributed to those functions.

Cost elimination as a critical action comes about only because it has been neglected as a continuing necessity. We get fat because we lose sight of our purpose and control. What exists has been done to us by ourselves.

To remedy this, it is necessary to approach cost elimination in an entirely different manner. It must be a constant function through which management's performance is measured. It must be equitably administered.

Present cost-elimination programs fail because they are dull and painful. Honest managers find themselves faced with the same across-the-board cuts that the more experienced budget padders can easily survive. Each cost revolution exposes the fact that the management does not have a consistent attitude of cost elimination.

While concern for cost is a primary factor in management, this concern is sometimes clouded by difficulty in recognizing opportunities for improvement. We get to know so much about our business that we lose the capacity to view it objectively. We may feel that what already surrounds us must always be; and worse, we may decide that we already are as cost-conscious as it is possible to be.

Take the matter of travel. Many companies insist that their executives travel tourist class in order to save the additional fare. Nobody who flies regularly likes the uncomfortable seats, the hurried service, and the overall humiliation that goes with tourist. The victim arrives at the destination disgruntled and certainly not in a company mood.

However, if you challenge a person to provide cost-elimination suggestions equivalent to 50 percent of the airfare over the year, with the provision of flying first class anyway, you will come out ahead. That will create something to think about on the plane. Staff troubleshooter types can be challenged to pick up a cost elimination on each trip equivalent to the total price of expenses, in addition to their regular task. They'll love it. . . .

Why Be Interested in Cost Elimination?

If you aren't, who will be?

The history of most companies shows a pattern of growth followed by slowing followed by growth and so on through the generations. What isn't shown so clearly is that interest in cost elimination is inversely proportional to the position of the cycle the company is enjoying. When everything is going great, expansion and risk are the buzz words. With the first recognizable sign of letdown—the ax starts swinging. Cost-reduction objectives are immediately established, and grim-faced executives tearfully tear the operation apart to reach those goals. This traumatic experience creates such an internal disturbance that the company may feel an additional self-produced reduction cycle before recovering. At any rate, the survivors will never look at the company or its management in the same way as before. I don't need to be too explicit—we have all been through it.

But if the managers are cost-elimination conscious at all times, the company will never get fat. The problem is to make this attitude happen during times of plenty, so that you never get caught with your costs up.

Thus cost elimination must be a continuous and personal program that is never neglected for more attractive and temporary pursuits.

What Causes Unnecessary Cost Increases?

Consider this question in reverse. What do you do when costs must be cut dramatically? You chop up the organization, condense the jobs to be done, eliminate people, wipe out branch offices, and, in general, pull everything together into a tighter, more cost-conscious environment. This must mean that you got a little carried away in the first place.

This thought applies to a total company problem. Most of us aren't concerned with that. But if you think of it on the basis of a department operation, or even a group, the pattern is the same. When cost-reduction time comes, we suddenly find that we have been oriented toward unending growth. Our personnel discussions have been concerned only with development and promotion.

Cost acceleration is also an attitude.

But the basic thing that causes costs to increase is lack of attention to their growth. As an earnest but inadequate golfer, I can state factually that almost all the trouble in my game stems from removal of the head from over the ball. Knowing this does not automatically eliminate the problem. Systematic discipline is required. Those who can enforce self-discipline are successful. Those who can't never get to cash in their stock options.

What Is the Difference Between Prevention, Elimination, and Reduction?

Cost Prevention.   This is a result of evaluating a situation so thoroughly before getting involved that you don't spend the money unless the result is sure to be profitable. Sometimes managers play games with this category by saying things like: "I decided not to paint the factory, so I'm putting in a savings of $56,000" or "I didn't buy that Rolls." This usually comes under the heading of cost avoidance.

Cost prevention is a continuing evaluation of new projects, hiring, organization expansion, and similar operations in a manner that makes them prove their own worth. It is obvious that hiring $100,000 worth of sales reps to produce $90,000 worth of sales may not be worthwhile in the long run. But it may not be so obvious that reorganization to create three new department heads may result in the elimination of only three people from the work pool while creating a source of no-profit-making overhead.

Cost Elimination.   To eliminate is to get rid of for good. Take the matter of a product that loses money. It is inevitable that many people will point out that this product is required in order to complete the line or satisfy special customers or serve some other very good purposes. You already know all of them.

However, looked at in the cold light of day, the product is a loser. Only three possible steps exist: raise the price so that you can make a proper profit, reduce the cost of producing it for the same reason, or get rid of it.

Usually cost reduction (and I'm getting ahead of myself) isn't going to work on this product, so you should consider the other things. If you really need the product, have your competitor make it for you and let them lose the money.

Cost elimination is based on the thought of "Do we need it at all?" rather than "Can we become more efficient?" or "Is this the best approach?" Much has been written about functions that were established for very good reasons and then outlived their usefulness. I'm sure that somewhere in the federal government, there is still a bureau of stagecoach regulation.

I recommend that you provide each of your key managers with a handsomely mounted bullet suitable for biting. This will serve as a reminder, and you can check their cost-elimination effectiveness by walking around now and then checking for teeth marks.

Cost Reduction. This is like a diet. And like diets, cost reduction is usually accomplished on a crash basis. The success or failure of the project is measured by attaining the lower weight, or expense, set as the target. Like a diet, it is uncomfortable, unnatural, and usually temporary. Your doctor will tell you to lose 15 pounds, but you have no control over which 15 will disappear.

The most effective cost-reduction methods are those approached in a deliberate manner. Value analysis is a practical technique for those who take the time to understand it. It also generates an attitude of improving what you already have. Therefore, apply the elimination test first, and you may save yourself some trouble.

The key to cost reduction is establishing measurable goals and monitoring the progress toward them during the length of the program. But the goals must be specific. The absolutely worst one you can select is an across-the-board cut of some sort. It is unfair, impractical, and generally ineffective. You will get the reduction, but most of your time will be spent in granting exemptions.

Can You Establish Cost Elimination as a Continuing Attitude?

Certainly. It is well known that people concentrate on the things they think are important to their leaders. If cost prevention is a sometime thing with them, it is because they feel that it is a sometime thing with top management. They need constant reminders.

There is no reward for being frugal in a growing operation. There is no recognition of proper budget administration. There is no incentive to spend the money properly. Now be honest about it. Is there really any reward within your area of responsibility for running a tight ship? Think about the people who work for you. If they live within their budgets, do you ever mention it?

To make intelligent people cost-elimination conscious, you have to help them recognize that it is an important part of their job. Important to you and important to their superiors. Of course, if you're going to say it is important, you really have to believe it is. You can't fake it.

If neglect is the primary contributor to increased cost, the lack of imaginative approaches to cost elimination must certainly be an equal factor. Frankly, cost reduction isn't any fun, and cost prevention is looked upon as a personal affront by most people.

But it doesn't have to be that way. Cost elimination can be a useful and purposeful involvement. It can be a morale booster instead of a buster that produces sourpuss reactions and very little cash return.

The BAD program is an example of a way that cost reduction can be accomplished to everyone's advantage. BAD, meaning "Buck A Day," has been proved effective in every test made. It has been conducted by several thousand companies in all types of industries and situations. It is even done in England and Germany with the same success pattern.

BAD is a 30-day program that asks people to look at their jobs and offer ideas that will reduce the cost of doing each job by one dollar a day. The desired result is $250 from each employee; the BAD efforts of one thousand employees will produce a fast quarter of a million dollars.

The program is cleverly put together, I will note with all due modesty. It communicates through good humor and plays on the word BAD. BAD is Good. BAD makes cents. And so forth. The teaser campaign features mysterious footprints and hints that "the BAD guys are coming."

Everyone submitting an idea wins a prize, and every prize is the same: a cup labeled "I had a BAD idea." Currently, the program is being used by hospitals seeking some effective way to reduce costs. It has been an outstanding success, producing at least ten times cost returns.

BAD is good.

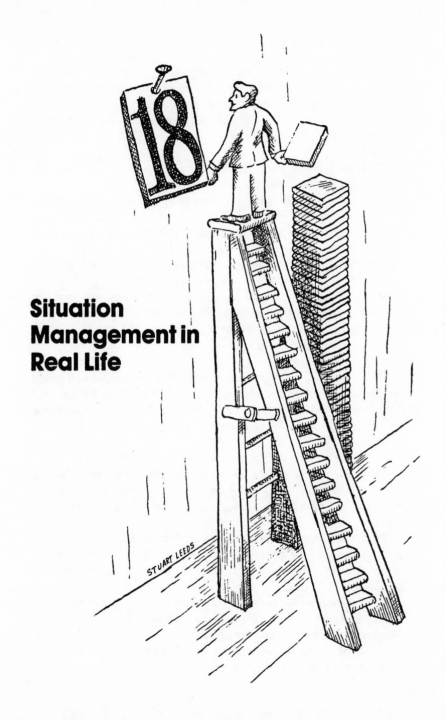

**Situation
Management in
Real Life**

STUART LEEDS

Wouldn't it be nice if there really were planned conspiracies to keep us from meeting our goals? What if the government had a department dedicated to interfering with our personal plans in such a way that nothing happened as we wished? What if the big corporations really were smart enough to foil each attempt we made to succeed? Oh, wouldn't it be loverly?

Then we could sit back, sigh in resignation, and give up the whole mess. "No use," we could say, "they've got us outflanked."

I know it sounds a little silly, but most of us believe that at least some of it's true. Haven't you heard the stories about the little guy who invented a carburetor that would produce 100 miles per gallon of gasoline and the oil companies bought him out and shut him up? Or the golf ball that would let everyone drive 300 yards? Or the fabric that never wears out? Or a hundred other things along that line?

When the Alaskan pipeline was completed, it became apparent that the cost of getting the crude oil to the refineries in Texas or the East Coast was going to be outlandishly expensive. Also the Californians didn't want any more installations like that on their coast. Everything became a big problem.

Then somebody had the idea of shipping that oil to Japan and having the Mideast oil Japan had contracted for sent directly to the East and Gulf Coasts in the United States. It would be less expensive for everyone, and oil is oil; you can't tell Alaskan crude from Saudi crude after it becomes gasoline.

Nobody even let them get past the end of the first sentence. "Send our oil to Japan? Never!" So we are still in the same situation. Nobody wants to build refineries in their town. Nobody wants to let pipelines be installed. And most of all, nobody wants to send "our" oil out of the country.

All of the people involved at every level of this mess feel that there is a conspiracy at the other levels to keep them from getting what they want. Actually, there is just a lack of mutual understanding and compassion.

Take the matter of behavior-modification drugs. If you bring up that subject at a cocktail party, you will receive a lecture on how drugs are being smuggled into the country and sold to kids. "That is why they all have this problem. The government should get tougher, close the borders, and put pushers in jail."

All of those are probably worthwhile, if useless, acts. The number of people in jail is related only to how many jail cells are available. But the question is: How come the kids are the ones who get all the attention and the government gets all the blame? After all, the best-selling drugs are adult drugs: alcohol, Valium, and sleeping pills. Children learn about drugs and their pleasures from their parents. They tend to see little difference between a cocktail party and a "shoot-up" session. Except, perhaps, that cocktail-party people are better dressed.

The bottom line of any concept very clearly relates to the realistic usefulness of it to you as an individual. What good is learning something if it won't do you any good? Why change your lifestyle around if you don't wind up being more comfortable? We don't need one more thing to fail at.

What sort of strategies could you develop to resolve some of the family's more pragmatic problems? What questions need to be answered? What sorts of things should you think about?

To Move or Not to Move

Americans have always been a highly mobile people. Today it is considered a routine part of career and life to move several times during your active life. The sunbelt states grow while the industrial northern cities are shrinking—but it was the other way around not too long ago. Sometimes trends are really fads; it is hard to know what to think when moving seems to be such a casual event.

The major reason for transplanting a family from one location to another is usually an improved career opportunity for one of the family members. With two or more adult wage earners now the typical situation in families, this can mean that one of them may be faced with losing a career opportunity. This can produce internal tensions that cannot be repaired with mere money and status. There are no easy decisions along this line, but there is a way to make it come off with less pain: Let the decision be the family's, not just one person's.

I think a family should never move for money alone. A bigger, better house, a new brand of suits, a longer vacation, and the increased money disappears as though it never existed. You can get used to anything.

Families should only move for increased opportunity—whether

career, education, culture, freedom, or something that by itself is good for the future of the family. Going back to where relatives live so you can have a more comfortable social base can be something that makes the family grow and prosper; conversely for some families, leaving that base provides a chance to grow that had previously been stifled.

So the question should be: "What is the best decision for the family's future?" The vital aspects are growth opportunity in social, educational, cultural, and career functions. It helps you little to triple your salaries if you have to spend your time sitting on an iceberg staring at a seal.

Planning and Education Budget for the Family

Someone in every family, nowadays, has to become an expert on scholarships. Millions of dollars are available for scholarships to anyone who appears to be serious about their education. College people tell me that they have a hard time filling them each year.

Such things are real and should be taken into consideration when planning the student's high school program. Make certain the proper subjects are taken and make certain that the student takes things like grades seriously. That is all that is essential, unless of course you can arrange to be 250 pounds and run the 100-yard dash in 9.3 seconds. For that you don't need grades.

It is not proper for a family executive to rely solely on the whims of scholarship committees. Education is too important to leave to chance. It is best to have a family program for tuition assistance. Setting money aside is something that requires discipline, as you already know; where you put that money is an entirely different matter. Many people place regular funds in savings accounts, money market funds, or stocks only to find that they have to pay income tax on the interest at the tax rate of the breadwinners. That eats up the fund. There are better ways, and brokers as well as banks can assist you.

For instance: Buy annuities in the child's name; there is no income tax due until the money is withdrawn, and then not until you have drawn out what you put in. Set up a "Clifford Trust" (this lets you give them the income from stock, property, etc. and have the principal returned intact in 10 years). U.S. Savings Bonds are good too. There are a lot of ways to make interest tax-free, at least for a while.

It adds up. Take the interest rate you are getting and divide it into

72. That tells you how many years it takes to double. So if you invest $5000 at 9 percent, and don't have to pay tax on the interest until you use it, it will be worth $10,000 in 8 years, $20,000 in 16 years, and so on.

My thought is that the family should pay for tuition and legitimate school expenses. The student should work and pay for everything else from pizzas to automobiles.

Settling Budget Allocations for the Family

No subject has more information and less control than budgets. Most families concentrate on bookkeeping, or keeping track, rather than defining where and for what money should be expended. It is this aspect that causes the emotionalism in discussions. No one is ever at fault; it is always the unplanned that does us in.

What we need is a change of attitude, not a better system of accounting. "Keeping neat records of overspending is not money management."

Money management, not budget control, that is the name of the game. Very few family managers bother to take one of the free courses offered by banks or civic organizations, courses aimed at understanding the concept of money management, not necessarily the techniques. Many family managers think they are doing well by their family when they continually pay for repairing the washing machine rather than buying a new unit with a warranty. However, a cost analysis might show that it would be less drain on the family resources to have regular payments instead of those surprises every month, besides having the washing machine out of service.

The point is that there are many ramifications of how to use the money. Everyone has been through the "rent or buy" decision. They usually buy based on all kinds of things from building equity to tax deductions, but the real reason may be to lower the hassle factor by eliminating the landlord.

I never knew anyone, including myself, who could manage their financial relationship by putting the funds in different envelopes (or accounts) and spending out of them. I guess we have all tried that. It just doesn't work because you can't see the whole package from there. The view is too narrow and limited.

Since Dr. Parkinson has shown that expenditure rises to meet income, and I can vouch for that, I shall try to provide one rule of family financial management. Take 10 percent off the top of whatever you receive and invest it where it is hard to get at but pays a fair and safe return; take the next 10 percent and give it to the Lord's work with a willing heart; and spend the rest.

Resolving Family Conflicts

Family disagreements have one more problem than all other discussions—the emotional involvement. It all gets very personal. No one really listens to each other in a family brawl, because there are a lot of very important things involved in the solution. The winner gains pecking order points over the loser.

The Situation Analysis strategy system is useful to many family and personal decisions. Suppose you have a brand new licensed driver who wants the car to go out on a date. Suppose you also have the mother of the brand-new licensed driver who is laying down rules concerning taking the car out. There is bound to be some disagreement.

Mother will want the car and its occupants back inside the garage by 9:30 P.M. Son will think that 2 A.M. is entirely reasonable.

Mother will expect that the car be used on nights when there is no school or other obligation in the morning. Son will request that it be available every night that something important is going to happen.

Mother will request that the car not be driven on the freeways because the traffic speed is so high that the inexperienced driver can be in real danger.

Son will require permission to drive on the freeways since that is the most efficient way to get anywhere and reduces the total time of the trip, thus eliminating any danger.

Mother will require that the driver pay all gasoline and support bills associated with use of the vehicle.

Son will suggest that any such expenses incurred can be traded off against lawn work, which will then be done at increased prices.

The only way to solve such an impasse without repeating it every day is for the family executive to draw up two questionnaires listing the items under dispute. All parties affected fill in the blanks and submit their opinions to judgment. The FE works out a compromise based on general practice, good sense, and the rules of safety. "Privileges given for responsibility shown" type of thing. All emotion is removed. The resulting document is discussed with the participants and all involved sign it because they have agreed in advance to arbitration. Any points which make one unhappy can be reviewed after a set period of time.

The document is then affixed in an accessible spot, there to remain for reference and problem solving. The same process can be utilized as the age, needs, and number of the participants change. It serves as a base for the next new drivers as they appear.

Getting Satisfaction from a Supplier

Everything you read about dealing with a supplier when you have a problem has to do with getting them straightened out one way or another after they have given you a problem. Most methods work to some extent, but you never really become whole again, even if the product or service finally comes across. It is a difficult world for the typical family because their individual buying power is just not enough to make or break a supplier. However there is a way to cut some of your pain by preventing problems rather than just trying to fix them after the fact.

If you can deal with a supplier enough to make a personal relationship with them, you have a better chance of success. A great many of our purchasing problems come from trying to save a buck by going to a place we have never been to before.

Industrial buyers, and the quality control people who are involved with purchasing for large companies, have learned a bitter lesson about purchasing in the past few years. The tried and true method of purchasing has always been to tell several suppliers what you were interested in buying, get bids from them, and pick the lowest one. When the product would arrive at the facility, the quality control people would inspect it to see if it was what they ordered. The idea was that if there was anything wrong, it would be returned and they would start over.

In most cases, however, it would turn out that there wasn't enough time to send that box back and get a new one, so judgments had to be made about using the nonconforming material. Elaborate systems of material review were developed, rework was made into a special skill, and somehow the products got used.

It is just too late to do much about it when you have run out of time and money. The same laws take effect on the far end of your personal production line—you have to go off to work whether you want to or not.

What is being learned is that prevention must be a big part of every purchase. First, the purchasers must know what they want and transmit that knowledge to the supplier. The two must then agree on those requirements, and both of them must take the requirements very seriously.

All of this eliminates the need for resting your whole fate on a receiving inspection of some kind. It puts the responsibility for action up front when something can be done about things, and cuts down the activity at the end when little or nothing can be done.

Is this just an interesting thought? Is it practical for the family to try to do something about their purchasing, to try to get the suppliers prevention-oriented? Is your buying power too insignificant?

Multiply your annual income by 40 years, and you will see that the family deals with an incredible amount of money. $25,000 a year with no inflation increases, is a million dollars over that time. You are not a nickel-and-dime purchaser—you have real clout.

There is no reason that consumers should have most of the problems they have. If you find a purchasing agent somewhere and press the point, you will learn that the company feels they cause half the problems and the supplier causes the other. Therefore, it isn't enough to change suppliers every time something goes wrong. In a small town, you'll be out of grocery stores before long.

Eliminating Hassle in the Family

My unofficial, biased, and personally conducted surveys show clearly that the biggest problem between generations is that one (usually the younger) doesn't take the advice and guidance offered by the other (usually the older).

The quarrels seem to have little to do with the advice itself in terms of its worth. After all, if you give counsel on every subject that comes up, you are bound to hit one now and then that you're right about.

Junior members of the family are given advice and direction on every single portion of life, much of it overstated and a great deal erroneous.

"Don't climb there, you'll break your neck." "If you ride the bike that way, you'll get run over by a car." "Don't be like that, people won't like you."

All of these are terminal thinking. "Break your neck," "run over by a car," "not like you" are all the extremes of the situation. As such expressions become common, the youngster learns that most warnings never come true and are, in fact, dishonest creations of an adult trying to gain their own sweet way without working at it.

Eventually, a credibility gap appears; it becomes clear that Mom and Dad as well as everyone else in authority exaggerates. Once you figure that out, you know that you don't have to take everything they say to heart. However, being young and inexperienced, this means that you can't tell the difference between advice that is important and advice that is not. Thus, the chief killer of young people is the automobile used improperly. They feel that no harm can come to them, that the laws of physical science do not apply in their case.

Overcoming all of this requires a discipline and understanding on the part of the family executive that really stretches human limitation. But it can be developed and applied in some cases, perhaps enough to prevent the disasters that you know will occur when proper advice is not accepted.

To head it all off, simply do not offer advice unless it is asked for. Establish the rules of the family, the do's and don'ts that make up the structure of the operation, then notify each member that you will not give advice, but you will answer every question.

As an example, one of the rules would be that everyone has to go to college, and when they pick one they have to stay there. No dropping out to "find themselves"—that they can do on their own time later. But the student gets to pick the college and the major. The family will not interfere.

The rule then is: "I will not give you advice unless asked, and I will not criticize you if you ask for advice."

Think about it: We tell them about the Easter Bunny, Santa Claus, the tooth fairy, and such without letting them know that these are all delightful fables. We lie to them about where babies come from, we hide our real interfamily relationships from them to "protect" them because they wouldn't understand. How can they understand anything if they aren't permitted to share the real things of life?

Situation management in real life is working hard to understand and then working harder to explain. Movies of traffic accidents and even trips to the morgue will not keep teenagers from taking chances when driving, but an honest relationship with an adult they respect will. Achieving that . . . well, that is what family management is all about.

Guidelines for Browsers

Index

Catalog